What Every Professional Organizer
Needs to Know About
HOARDING

Judith Kolberg

Squall Press™

What Every Professional Organizer Needs to Know About
Hoarding

Copyright© 2008 by Judith Kolberg

ISBN 978-0-9667970-5-3

Squall Press™ books may be ordered through booksellers or by
contacting:

Squall Press
P. O. Box 691
Decatur, GA. 30031
404-231-6172
www.squallpress.net
info@squallpress.net

Photo credits: Jonda Beattie
Text, cover design and editing: Wolfmont LLC
Back cover photo: Leland Holder, Lelandonlocation.com

Squall Press is a division of FileHeads Professional Organizers

Printed in the United States of America

Acknowledgment

There are two people, without which, this book would never have been written; Heidi Schulz who instigated the idea and Tony Burton of Wolfmont, LLC who hammered draft after draft into a final product. Julie Bestry's research was as on-point and thorough as I could ever hope for. David Tolin's support truly moved me to make it a book that reached beyond professional organizers. Organizers, Randi Lyman, Lynne Johnson, Mo Osborn, and Lynn Mino provided key on-the-front-lines perspective for which I am very grateful. I would like to thank hoarding specialists Henriette Kellum, Irene Tobis and Kristin Bergfeld for contributing their unique point of view. And old friends, Ann Gambrell and Sandra Felton proved again there is no limit to their giving. It was a delight to talk things through with Catherine Roster. I am very grateful to Diane Smith for her read of the draft. Many thanks to the NSGCD for their sustained work on this tough problem and for keeping a place for me at the table.

Dedication

This book is dedicated to those wonderful people who refuse to let the overwhelming challenges of clutter and disorganization rob them of humor, kindness and intelligence. And to the persistence of professional organizers, researchers, and therapists who are committed to making a difference.

Praise for
WHAT EVERY PROFESSIONAL ORGANIZER NEEDS TO KNOW ABOUT HOARDING

"Judith Kolberg's previous book, *Conquering Chronic Disorganization*, helped me to see the problem of hoarding from a different angle. In this book, she describes how professional organizers and mental health professionals can team up. I suspect this book will be inspirational and informative for organizers who find themselves struggling with clients who hoard. I am particularly hopeful that this work will pave the way toward increased collaboration between organizing and mental health professionals, so that both groups can bring their unique perspectives and skill sets to help those who suffer from this common and debilitating disorder."

-- David F. Tolin, Ph.D., Director,
Anxiety Disorders Center, Institute of Living

"Kolberg has done it again. Her book about hoarding brings hope to anyone who works with or loves a compulsive, excessive saver. I'm recommending it to all my colleagues."

--Standolyn Robertson, Former President,
National Association of Professional Organizers

"Judith Kolberg draws on her experience to clearly present the problem of hoarding and its remediation. Digging through confusion and distress, she opens the windows of thought for a fresh look at how hoarders can be helped. This book is a very useful tool for anyone, professional or not, who wants to help someone suffering with this problem."

-- Sandra Felton, The Organizer Lady®, founder of Messies Anonymous (www.messies.com), author of
The Messies Manual and *Organizing for Life*

"Once again, Kolberg has brought her expertise and uncanny insight to bear on a serious topic of growing importance. This book is a must-read, not only for professional organizers, but all those who work with hoarders and whose lives are affected by this complex and often life-crippling condition."
-- Catherine A. Roster, Ph.D., Associate Professor, Marketing, University of New Mexico

"*What Every Professional Organizer Needs To Know About Hoarding* is a gold mine of information! It gives the organizers tools we need to assess situations with our clients; both current and prospective. I know this book will be a valuable resource for me."
-- Diane N. Quintana, Staff Professional Organizer, Parkaire Consultants, Inc., Owner DNQ Solutions

"This book will be eagerly received by the professional organizing community. It provides a comprehensive overview of one of the most challenging types of work we encounter. It also brings hope and encouragement to individuals who hoard and those who care about them - family members, friends, communities, and professionals in other fields. Judith has once again created an important resource that needs to be part of every professional organizer's library."
-- Lynne Johnson, CPO-CDR®, NSGCD Master Trainer, Former President, National Study Group on Chronic Disorganization

"This book will raise the bar for all organizers by expanding their awareness and understanding of the complex emotional and environmental challenges of the hoarder."
-- Heidi Schulz, CPO-CD® & Roland Rotz, Ph.D., Collaborative Therapy for Clutter Management

"Sooner or later every professional organizer will walk into the life of a hoarder. Take the job or not? How to help, not harm? Where to turn for support? In her usual thorough, insightful, and very readable style, Kolberg touches all the bases and leaves the reader empowered to face these always daunting situations."
-- Valentina Sgro, award-winning author and speaker, www.reallyorganized.com

"With her keen observation and positive, non-judgmental attitude, Kolberg discovered effective ways to help chronically disorganized people long before compulsive hoarding was recognized as a psychological disorder. She is a pioneer in encouraging therapists and professional organizers to work together. I continue to use her insights in my own work on a daily basis."

-- Irene Tobis, former organizer, Ph.D., Psychologist, Specializing in compulsive hoarding, The Austin Center for the Treatment of Obsessive-Compulsive Disorder, www.austinocd.com

"Vital reading for any professional organizer or layperson that has ever or will ever venture to help someone with hoarding tendencies. In her matter-of-fact and often humorous style, Judith provides for us a treasure of resources. "

-- Jana Hartwell, Founder and President of *Sensible Organizing Solutions, Inc.* (www.sensibleorganizing.com), Past President of NAPO-San Diego, CA

"I appreciate the timeliness of this book. There are professional organizers at the top of our profession who lack the knowledge to work appropriately and effectively with this complex group. This book is a much needed resource that addresses critical issues we need to understand. Thank you, Judith Kolberg for writing about a much misunderstood condition."

-- Randi B. Lyman, CPO-CD®, Publication Director, National Study Group on Chronic Disorganization

Foreword

I am delighted to write the foreword for
Judith Kolberg's new book. The concept of chronic
disorganization emerged from the field of
professional organizing around the same time as
my colleagues in psychology and psychiatry were
noting, with increased interest, a phenomenon they
termed *compulsive hoarding*.

Although not officially recognized by the
*Diagnostic and Statistical Manual of Mental Disorders,
4th Ed-Text Revision* (DSM-IV-TR), we currently
define compulsive hoarding as the acquisition
(buying, picking up free things) of a large number
of possessions that appear to be useless or of
limited value; failure to discard possessions (e.g.,
difficulty making critical decisions about whether
to keep or discard); and clutter that precludes
activities for which living spaces were designed
(e.g., inability to cook in the kitchen, eat in the
dining room, sleep in the bedroom, move through
the home, etc.). Personally (although Judith may
not completely agree with me on this point), I

suspect that the phenomena of chronic disorganization and compulsive hoarding overlap substantially, and in many cases we may be using different terminology to describe the same thing. A recent epidemiologic study by Johns Hopkins University suggested that the prevalence of hoarding may be as high as 5%, or one out of every 20 people.

Regardless of what we call it, we know that this phenomenon can cause serious problems in functioning. Social service workers are all too familiar with the risks of fire, falling, poor sanitation and exacerbation of medical conditions caused by excessive clutter. My colleagues Randy Frost and Gail Steketee surveyed health department officials and found that in 6% of hoarding cases, clutter was judged to contribute directly to the individual's death in a house fire.

Even in less dramatic cases, individuals who hoard generally report high levels of depression, social isolation, and functional impairment. We recently surveyed several hundred self-reported hoarders, who reported a level of work impairment (which we defined as the number of days removed from the workforce due to illness) that equaled or exceeded that seen in most anxiety and depressive disorders, and was comparable to those seen in conditions such as bipolar disorder or schizophrenia. Family members seem to suffer as well: our survey found that growing up in a hoarding home was associated with unhappy childhoods, reduced social activity, increased family conflict, and highly negative attitudes toward the hoarder.

For a long time, we thought that compulsive hoarding was a subtype of obsessive-compulsive disorder (OCD). Although this question is far from resolved, research suggests that compulsive hoarding may not be specifically associated with OCD, but rather may be a feature of a range of psychiatric disorders including schizophrenia, social phobia, organic mental disorders, eating disorders, depression, and dementia.

Furthermore, OCD patients usually display some recognition that their obsessive thoughts and compulsive behaviors are irrational and maladaptive; in contrast, we have found that many patients with compulsive hoarding report surprisingly little distress or recognition of the problem. In addition, studies of OCD treatment outcome have consistently shown hoarding symptoms to be a predictor of poor outcome for standard OCD treatments, suggesting that compulsive hoarding and OCD may involve different biological, cognitive, or behavioral mechanisms.

A theoretical model is emerging that suggests multiple potential causes of hoarding behavior. Core vulnerability factors such as negative beliefs about the self, preexisting psychiatric disorder, parental environment, significant loss, and genetic factors may "set the stage" for the development of hoarding later in life. Information-processing deficits, such as difficulty with attention, memory, categorization, and decision-making, hamper the individual's capacity to effectively organize and discard possessions. Maladaptive beliefs about possessions further hijack the decision-making process; these can include emotional attachment to possessions, memory-related concerns, responsibility for possessions, and excessive need for control over possessions.

We are still in the early stages of learning how to treat compulsive hoarding. It seems clear from the available evidence that medications are not the answer for most people, at least not the medications that have been tested so far. It is certainly possible (and I remain hopeful) that future research will discover a medication or combination of medications that can produce a meaningful and sustainable reduction in hoarding behavior.

We are obtaining better results with a form of counseling called *cognitive-behavioral therapy*, which is characterized by strategies to enhance the client's motivation to change, helping the client to understand how their hoarding behaviors are maintained, teaching effective decision-making, and helping the client learn to resist impulses to acquire. Our research thus far suggests that 50-60% of clients are considered "much improved" or "very much improved" after 6 months of treatment. While we find this encouraging, and certainly better than the results obtained with medications in past studies, we are also realistic about the limitations of the treatment. First, 40-50% of clients simply do not appear to respond very well to the treatment. Second, we are keenly aware that "improvement" is not the same thing as "cure." Even for our treatment "responders," most of them still had significant clutter and hoarding behaviors at the end of treatment (although the problem was certainly better managed and their quality of life substantially improved). Clearly, there is much room for improvement, and we need lots of smart people thinking about this problem.

Which brings us to the book you're holding. Judith Kolberg is a leading expert on the topic of chronic disorganization, and her previous book, *Conquering Chronic Disorganization*, helped me to see the problem from a different angle. In this book, Judith supplies several case examples that illustrate the phenomenon, and describes how professional organizers and mental health professionals can team up to address the problem.

I suspect that this book, and the ideas contained within, will be inspirational and informative for organizers who find themselves struggling with clients who hoard.

I am particularly hopeful that this work will pave the way toward increased collaboration between organizing and mental health professionals, so that both groups can bring their unique perspectives and skill sets to help those who suffer from this common and debilitating disorder.

David F. Tolin, Ph.D.
Director, Anxiety Disorders Center, Institute of Living
Adjunct Associate Professor of Psychiatry,
Yale University School of Medicine
Author, *Buried in Treasures: Help for Compulsive Acquiring,
Saving and Hoarding*

Preface

"Hoarder"… the word itself conjures up an image of a miserly individual, isolated from society in a cave of clutter. It would be nice if there were a better word for a person who hoards. "Excessive saver" cleans it up too much and the word "hoarder" sounds indicting. This book will teach you what hoarding is so that when you hear the word, you'll know about the syndrome it describes and will be able to get past the word itself. Why is it important for you to know about hoarding? Because every professional organizer will encounter a person who hoards, whether you are new, experienced, work in residential settings, or work in business environments.

It is important to know what to do when you encounter a hoarder, even if your final decision is not to work with that individual as a client. You may already have an organizing niche with which you are satisfied. That's fine. It is admirable to define and pursue a career in organizing that is distinct and independent of other disciplines. We need the industry of organizing to continue to sophisticate, clarify and be credible in its own right.

This book will teach you how to recognize hoarding, what to do if you find yourself figuratively (or literally!) over your head, and how to opt out of working with a person who hoards in an ethical way so that the hoarding individual has other options. If you are unsure if working with hoarding clients is for you, this book will help you make that assessment. For the more veteran organizer looking for a professional challenge, this book takes you right into the approaches that are proving to be most successful for engaging this complex issue but it is not a manual on how to implement a complex hoarding project. It is an overview of the complex problem of hoarding.

There are few cases of hoarding reported earlier than the Great Depression. Perhaps this is partially due to the fact that most Americans had little money to acquire excess stuff. One of the most notorious cases is that of the reclusive Collyer brothers. Homer Collyer was trained as an engineer, and Langley Collyer was an attorney. Living in their childhood home in Manhattan, they obsessively collected newspapers, books, furniture, musical instruments, baby carriages and even pickled human organs. Their gas, telephone, electricity and water were turned off for failure to pay the bills. Langley left the house at night to obtain water from a park, returning home with abandoned items.

Interviewed by *The New York Herald Tribune* about the huge mounds of clutter, Langley explained, "I am saving newspapers for Homer, so that when he regains his sight he can catch up on the news." On March 21, 1947, police received an anonymous tip about a dead man in the Collyer brownstone. Noticing a foul odor emanating from the house, police tried to gain entry but were blocked by walls of clutter. They eventually broke in through a second-story bedroom, digging through walls of newspapers, packages, baby carriages and gardening implements for two hours before eventually reaching Homer, dead in his chair. Two and a half weeks later, a workman lifted piles of boxes, newspapers and luggage to find Langley's decomposing body. Langley had tried to crawl through a tunnel of newspapers to bring food to Homer when he triggered a booby trap, causing the junk to collapse upon him. Homer, blind, paralyzed and blockaded by squalor, eventually starved to death.

Not all people who hoard are like the Collyer brothers. Compulsive hoarding has degrees of severity. Depending on the severity, hoarding can cause accidents and can be a threat to life and limb if emergency responders cannot access the home. It drives away loved ones, stresses entire families, and contributes to divorce. It causes respiratory problems, aggravates allergies, disrupts sleep, and causes headaches. Neglected structural damage to homes causes safety issues, health hazards and infestations. Hoarding wreaks havoc on household budgets and drives people into debt.

The inability to comply with the basic obligations of being a responsible homeowner or renter and a good neighbor, has caused hoarders to be evicted from their homes or live under constant threat of eviction. The problem is coming to the public's attention none too soon.

As the population ages, the issue of hoarding grows more complex. Hoarding tendencies can begin in the teen years, but hoarding often does not manifest full-blown until people are in their 50's or later. Statistically, the incidence of hoarding will no doubt rise. Many older Americans are choosing to age-in-place; that is, continue to live in their homes as long as they are physically able.

In addition, since we are living longer and longer, our homes may be our residences for many more years than in past generations. We have more time to acquire more things. Aging-in-place is a good option for people who can rely on family, friends and support services to accommodate them in their home as they cope with less mobility, possible memory issues, balance problems, or other issues that accompany aging. With a good thirty years ahead of them, a hoarder at fifty will find aging-in-place wrought with so many significant health and safety issues that it may not be an option.

This book recognizes that a vast array of professionals in a wide-range of occupations (and many non-professionals) are acquainted with hoarding. These include: family members, attorneys, law enforcement, social workers, sanitation department employees, first responders, child protective agencies, insurance personnel, repairmen and contractors, animal welfare, guardians of the elderly, court systems, suicide hotlines, sheriff departments, divorce and custody courts, real estate agents, and, of course, mental health practitioners. I believe the information in this book will benefit anyone interested in improving the quality of life for a person who hoards. We all need to join forces.

Professional organizers occupy a special vantage point when it comes to the hoarding issue. We are in these individuals' home and offices, up close and personal with a first-hand account of their circumstances and the challenges they face. We have much to contribute to the complex solutions hoarding requires. We can:

- Work hands-on to help eliminate health and safety hazards, create cleared living spaces and return a home to a functioning level
- Identify health care services and foster collaboration.
- Be the eyes and ears for therapists and a part of a treatment plan for a person who hoards
- Provide organizing skill-training, decision-making and information-processing skills
- Encourage discard strategies, reduce clutter and mitigate its recurrence
- Consult with the client, their family and other "players" to develop an action plan for a hoarding project
- Rally, manage, and supervise supplemental services
- Experiment with, and document, effective organizing methods
- Blow the whistle in the case of life threatening situations

The opportunities available to use your own unique abilities are many. Working with people who hoard is challenging, stimulating and fulfilling, and will use every talent you have. Gaining knowledge about this complex client will give you greater career choice, deepen your organizing skills, benefit all your clients, and bring you into a larger network of colleagues in other professions. Most importantly, knowledge about hoarding will enable our profession to contribute to the improvement of the quality of life for individuals who hoard, something of which we can all be proud.

Table Of Contents

A Tale of Two Clients

Doris's Story

Janette is a competent, confident professional organizer. She's had three chronically disorganized clients who struggle with making the clutter go away and stay away. Janette is pretty creative about devising systems to meet her clients' needs, and prides herself on listening to her clients and involving them in the solution. She is compassionate when progress is slow or there is backsliding.

Doris, her latest client, is not a very good housekeeper. Taking that together with the clutter, it would be easy for Janette to feel that Doris is a lazy person, unconcerned about the comfort of others or that perhaps she doesn't understand simple organizing principles like getting rid of stuff that's not needed. But Janette is a professional and has learned not to be judgmental. Instead, she puts her feelings aside and stays focused on the organizing task at hand.

Recently, she and Doris set about dealing with papers and the mail. The mail was heaped high on the dining room table and made it impossible to enjoy meals there. Together they sat down on the sofa and sorted through a representative stack of mail. Janette made a list of the junk mail Doris wanted stopped and with her permission, sent a letter requesting her name and address be removed from the third-class mail database.

Janette encouraged new habits for Doris like sorting the mail with a trash can nearby so it could be discarded immediately. They set up a designated place to sort the mail, and Janette and she created mail cubbies for each family member. Janette transferred to Doris other excess-reducing skills like ignoring solicitations for donations and instead determining in advance which charities to support and sticking with them.

Some of the dialogue went like this:

"Tell me about all these receipts," Janette asks as she observes hundreds of receipts from grocery stores, department stores, and restaurants.

"I might need to return something to the store," Doris responds, certain of her reasoning.

Janette challenges her logic. "How often do you return things to the store, would you say?"

"Maybe once or twice a year."

"And is it usually groceries?"

"No, never."

"Well, then you can let go of the grocery receipts. Are the restaurant receipts for business purposes?"

"No."

"They can be tossed too." Sensing Doris might be a little overwhelmed with this much change, they compromised and agreed to hold all receipts for one month, except department store receipts which would be held for six months. Doris is frugal and prides herself on saving money. She holds onto a lot of junk mail because of the coupons. Not terribly computer-savvy, Doris cannot search for them online when she needs them. Janette and Doris agree that for 3 months, until she can get the mail under control, she'll ignore the coupons. Later, when the new habits are engrained and Doris feels she has control over the mail, saving coupons will make more sense.

To be honest, the dining room table is never cleared off completely. It's always a bit of a mish-mosh with mail, to-do lists, stationery supplies, and catalogs… and more than one unfinished project like pictures to frame, or a book to send to someone. Still, as the papers recede, the dining room table is less of an eyesore.

Janette notices papers and projects of every kind cluttering up Doris' house. They lie in small stacks on nearly every surface and fill cartons that occupy precious space in Doris' small house, but papers are the priority. Janette is aware Doris hates to deal with paper.

So she sits with her and they go through the backlog. It is a difficult, slow process requiring Doris to make a decision about the dispossession of each piece of paper. She has a good degree of worry about papers she might need again, and concern about information that can't be replaced or stuff to keep "just in case." Janette is able to give her a reality check on those common worries and concerns and little by little Doris becomes more secure about getting rid of excess and unwanted stuff.

It takes weeks but when it is over, Doris has discarded over ten big bags of trash, she has the semblance of a filing system, three large plastic bags of stuff to shred, four plastic bags of recycling and a system for handling the daily mail and receipts.

If it was up to Janette, she'd opt for one big toss-it-away category for the unneeded papers. Janette recycles at home but Doris is so keen on recycling it actually slows the sorting process down. Janette knows that shredding papers that reveal personal information like social security numbers and account numbers prevents identity theft. Doris insists on shredding anything with her address or name on it, information so public and available that nobody can protect it. So the process is slow, but with practice the pace increases and Doris becomes more and more assured about letting go.

Janette teaches Doris that when her needs and interests change, letting go of paper and clutter goes along with it. "Keep the treasures, toss out the trash," Janette says over and over to Doris. Doris learns to be more selective about what to keep and what to toss (with the exception of her frog collection; there her acquiring and saving habits have no bounds). She understands that attempting to read every weekly newsletter, keeping every greeting card, and being hyper-vigilant about keeping every financial statement is burdensome and unnecessary.

Doris is fast approaching age sixty and has many things she'd like to do with her time instead of sorting papers. Janette assures Doris that the credit card offer she wants or the newsletter article she was looking for may indeed be discarded and regretted afterwards. But the regret will be brief and the gains of clear space, more control and less clutter justify getting rid of excess even with this slight risk. Doris wants to keep the place maintained and arranges to organize with Janette once per month, more often during high-organizing seasons like tax time or the beginning of the school year.

Hope's Story

Janette gets a call from Hope. Hope describes herself on the phone as chronically disorganized. She found Janette's name on the internet. They talk briefly on the phone and Hope identifies her problem as too much residential clutter and papers: right up Janette's alley. When Janette arrives for her first organizing session she notices the yard is unkempt. The plants are dead in their pots. Cardboard boxes are teetering on the porch in stacks shoulder high. Dozens of bird feeders and bird houses hang from the trees.

Hope comes out the screen door with a big bag of bird seed. She greets Janette with a warm hello and smile, and turns her attention to feeding the birds. She chats about each one, calling each by name. Janette finds Hope to be a pleasant, giving person. Still, she wonders when they will go inside. Finally, Hope walks indoors with Janette behind her. There is a distinct odor of mold and mildew. As far as the eye can see there are stacks of boxes, newspapers and junk mail. They are jumbled up with what appears to be clothing or linens. There are books and magazines, batteries and CD's, picture frames and empty soda bottles, magic markers and candy wrappers, totes of every imaginable type, empty boxes and brand new hand-towels still in the package. Janette can barely walk, there is no place to sit down and she realizes in an instant that she needs to keep her shoulder bag on her shoulder.

Hope is a librarian, a profession requiring public contact and intelligence. Janette remembers her on the phone as cogent and motivated, though a bit talkative. She keeps all of Hope's good qualities in mind as she tries to reconcile the house with the person. Not wanting to give away her true sense of appall, Janette monitors her body language and facial expression.

Hope begins to tell Janette a story about each object she picks up: how she acquired it, what she likes about it or for whom it is intended. "Ready for the big tour?" Hope says gleefully. They step over more clutter and make their way to the rear of the house. More of the same. Janette briefly pokes her head in the bathroom and decides a bathroom break is out of the question.

Hope's bedroom is not as bad. At least the bed is clear of clutter and there is a pathway around the bedroom to the bathroom. Janette catches a glimpse of the kitchen and wonders how it could be that a person like Hope, gainfully employed, bright and engaging, and clean and neat in appearance, could let things get so far out of control. It just doesn't make sense. "Let's go outside and talk," Janette advises where at least there is a railing to lean against and the air will do her good.

In the short walk from the rear of the house to the porch, Janette decides that with time and lots of help, she can reduce the excess in Hope's home. She is experienced enough to realize that she couldn't possibly do it alone and must bring in assistance. And she is a smart enough business woman to know that she has to ask about Hope's resources to pay for a job this big.

In the back of her mind, she envisions

winning Hope's trust and doing the project over time with more assistance. Janette intuitively knows Hope is her own worst enemy. "We've got an hour or so left to the organizing session. Let's do some organizing and see how it goes. When we stop, I'll have a better idea where to go from here," Janette proposes. She takes a bottle of water from her pocketbook, takes a swig to fortify herself, and unloads her pocketbook on the front porch.

"I drink a lot of water, too. I'm very health conscious," Hope remarks as she smiles broadly. Janette wonders how Hope can consider herself health-conscious, and yet lives in such unhealthy surroundings.

"Stop it," Janette says to herself, aware that she is prone to psychoanalyzing things too much. Janette grabs a wad of papers from beneath her feet. Cockroaches and silverfish scamper off in all directions and Janette wishes she had on rubber gloves.

"Those are receipts I need for taxes," Hope explains. The wad contains receipts two years old, unopened junk mail, candy wrappers, a pen, and several pennies.

Janette thinks this will be easy since it's mostly rubbish. "This receipt is for groceries. It's not deductible unless the groceries are for making meals to entertain clients or are for a charitable donation."

"I might have to bring something back. Here, I'll take it and put it in the kitchen." Off Hope goes to shuttle her tiny parcel to the kitchen.

Janette continues, "This piece of junk mail is stained and two years old. They are asking you for a donation and they send you a new appeal for money several times a year. How 'bout we toss this one away?"

"I have a stack of those over here. I'll go through them before you come back again."

Janette does not like the sound of that. Really, there was no rational reason to keep that piece of mail. And in Janette's experience, people who struggle with getting organized don't do homework. There's no way she's going to go through junk mail solicitations. Janette is beginning to wonder if Hope is just fooling herself, and worse, trying to pull one over on Janette.

"Here's a plastic bag for the garbage," Hope says, holding open a small plastic bag for Janette to deposit the candy wrappers. Surely Hope doesn't believe that grocery store bags are going to contain the amount of trash in this house. Something tells her not to engage Hope on this issue. "Always looking for a pen," Hope explains as she turns to take the pen to some unknown location.

"How 'bout we start a box for stationery supplies so you don't have to run around putting them away?" Janette grabs a nearby empty box, plunks the pen inside, finds another and puts it in.

"That pen goes to the office," Hope declares.

And so it goes. At the end of the session Janette holds the small plastic grocery store bag with candy wrappers, a couple of tissues, and a sock with a hole in it. The stationery supply box now has two pens, one envelope, a couple of paper clips and two dried up markers. She gazes over the mountain of clutter. Not all of it is junk. That's what makes Hope's house even more mystifying to Janette.

She sees new sheets still in the shopping bag,

perfectly usable shoes, coins, DVD's, books, and even jewelry mixed in with trash. Janette thinks what she needs is bigger firepower. "Hope, I have an idea. I can bring in a couple of assistants, lots of big garbage bags, some dustpans and more boxes. We can get my assistants going on the trash while you and I fill up the boxes with stuff you want to keep. Then, once the trash is out, we can organize your keepers."

Hope responds, "I don't think we need that many people. I can go through the trash between now and when you come back. Let's set up another time to organize."

Janette thinks, "What have I gotten myself into?" At this rate, item by item, one candy wrapper at a time in two- or three-hour sessions, she'll never get this lady organized. Not wanting to convey her doubts and concerns, Janette agrees. Though a long-term project might be nice for her bank account, Janette is already dreading the idea of coming back and wonders if she is being fair to Hope.

EXERCISE

The following exercise is designed to bring into focus the distinction between clients who hoard and those who simply may be chronically disorganized. Look at the below list of characteristics. Based on the stories above, circle either 'Doris' or 'Hope' or both names if you think the characteristic applies.

Can You Tell the Difference Between Doris and Hope?

Progress is slow	Doris	Hope
Useful and useless stuff are all mixed together	Doris	Hope
Organizing is done, disorganization recurs, and organizing must be done over	Doris	Hope
Is able to develop routines and habits	Doris	Hope
Sees the value in systems even if it is hard to maintain them	Doris	Hope
Can designate places for designated things	Doris	Hope
Has space for eating, sleeping and relaxing	Doris	Hope
Readily learns new organizing skills	Doris	Hope
Cannot discard apparent trash	Doris	Hope
Tends to be frugal	Doris	Hope
May need regular maintenance	Doris	Hope
Can make organizing decisions and stick to them	Doris	Hope
Can turn intention (i.e., recycling) into action	Doris	Hope
Finds a reason to keep everything	Doris	Hope
Experiences regret about throwing things away but gets over it	Doris	Hope

You'll notice Doris and Hope share some characteristics, such as slow progress, recurring clutter and the need for on-going maintenance. There are also significant differences between them. Hope's living spaces for eating and sleeping are totally compromised by clutter. They no longer serve their purposes. Hope is unable to discard useless items or in some cases sheer trash. She seems attached to even the lowliest of stuff and it is undermining the healthy functioning of daily life.

Chronic Disorganization Versus Hoarding

Chronic disorganization is defined as: having a past history of disorganization in which self-help efforts to change have failed, quality of life due to disorganization is undermined, and there is a future expectation of disorganization

All people who hoard can certainly be classified as chronically disorganized. Their quality of life is undermined by disorganization, a critical part of the definition of chronic disorganization. Because the clutter is so overwhelming and the underlying causes of hoarding so difficult to overcome, repeated self-help efforts fail (although in less severe cases and/or with a great deal of support, there may be improvement.) With chronically disorganized people, *recurrence* of disorganization is a central concern. They dig out some and then it returns. With people who hoard, the issue is not so much recurrence as it is perpetual disorganization into the future. The most important feature chronically disorganized people and people who hoard share is an undermined quality of life.

Though people who hoard are chronically disorganized in this general sense, very few chronically disorganized people are hoarders. Hoarding is quite rare. Less than 2% of the population are identified as hoarders. Hoarding is qualitatively different than chronic disorganization. People who hoard have a special relationship with their clutter. Sure, many chronically disorganized people can be overly sentimental, or fear they might need something they really ought to toss away. And they can love and enjoy objects just for their own sake without utility or worth entering the picture.

For people who hoard, these sentimental attachments and fears are so intense it is actually less painful to keep stuff than to discard it. Over time, excessive saving of everything robs living space of its intended use. Quality of life deteriorates, including health, finances, relationships and shelter, as a direct effect of hoarding behaviors.

This is not the experience of people we commonly call chronically disorganized. Chronically disorganized people do not necessarily devolve into hoarding. Doris, in the story at the beginning of this chapter, left to her own devices, would find a way to hide the stuff when company comes to visit. She'll get stressed out looking for things she can't find. She may buy things new that she already owns because she can't find these items when she needs them. She could even be clueless about what goes where and it is very likely she doesn't like to spend time organizing.

A professional organizer may have to work with her again and again to get things organized.

But her kitchen is still a kitchen. The entire house is not one big closet. A repairman can come and fix things. Clutter is not a hazard to her health or safety. Doris can make organizing decisions, and with time and effort, stand by them. She is in control of her behavior.

Hope, the woman in the second story at the beginning of this chapter, is compelled to excessively save due to mistaken beliefs. Her emotions about her stuff get in the way so much she can't sort things, categorize things or part with them. Sometimes it seems like she can't even see her clutter. The rooms of her home have lost all their integrity. Each now is a container for her stuff. Sadly, much of it is not worth saving at all, let alone giving it control over her home. Her quality of life is on a downward slide she cannot control without help. She really can't help it.

The activity of organizing may not be the most powerful initial, single or long-term path to rectifying the situation for people like Hope who are compulsive hoarders. This is because their issue with disorganization cannot be addressed by improvements in level of organization alone nor by an exclusively skill-based approach. No matter how persistent, creative, compassionate or skillful you are, a person who hoards has problems that cannot be addressed only by organizing.

The Mental Health Side of Hoarding

C h a p t e r   T w o

"The reasons hoarders save stuff is not so dissimilar from you and I," notes Dr. Randy O. Frost. Dr. Frost is a professor of psychology at Smith College and the author of over 100 articles on hoarding and related topics.

"Hoarders save more things than non-hoarders, but interestingly, their reasons for saving are the same as everyone else's. People save things for three basic reasons. Some objects have sentimental value, usually through a connection to important life events. Other objects have instrumental value; that is we need them to fulfill some tangible purpose or to complete an activity. Still other things may have little sentimental or instrumental value, but we simply like them intrinsically. People who hoard use these same reasons for saving; they simply apply them to more things." — *Dr. Randy O. Frost*

> Saving becomes hoarding when the items that represent our transitory and temporary wants and needs, become permanent fixtures in our lives.

For people who hoard, saving stuff becomes *unreasonable*. Saving becomes hoarding when sentimentality is *not* selective and *every* item becomes favored. Saving becomes hoarding when items that have lost their utility, are broken, obsolete, redundant, or not useful anymore are not discarded. Saving becomes hoarding when items are acquired and saved to meet every contingency, imagined or real.

The result of excessive saving is a large quantity of clutter. Underneath that clutter, if you will excuse the pun, are mistaken beliefs or maladjusted thinking in the mind of the individual that cause the hoarding.

What Do Hoarders Believe?

What follows is a list of the kinds of beliefs hoarders may harbor that underlie the behavior of excessive saving and emotional attachment to objects. Like everyone else, each person who hoards is a unique individual with a personality all their own. Not all people who hoard harbor all of these beliefs. It varies from person to person. Your client may or may not express these beliefs to you:

- I might make a mistake or wrong decision and throw away something I may need later. I should avoid mistakes and wrong decisions by not throwing anything away.
- If something important or necessary is discarded it will be unavailable when needed. I cannot risk this.
- I believe every object has beauty or value and deserves to be preserved. I believe there is an opportunity in every object to fulfill its utility or usefulness.
- If I throw away a sentimental object it is the same as throwing away the memory that goes with it.
- It is my personal responsibility to prevent wastefulness. Discarding objects is being wasteful.
- Saving everything allows me to exert control over my environment and therefore, my life.
- I simply enjoy the images my things provoke, the dream of using it, its potential rather than its real usage.

There are also fairly common beliefs that

relate to information. These beliefs include:

- Keeping quantities of information like newspapers, magazines and papers allows me to keep up and not fall behind. Falling behind has bad memories for me. I need to avoid this.

- I save information to have the perfect answer, solution or information for anyone who might need it. It is important to me to be perfect in this way.

- There may be important facts, information or messages on the papers, documents, newspapers, and information I have. I don't know for sure so I keep them just in case.

- I can't rely on my memory so I rely on papers, documents, newspapers, and information.

Some beliefs are more emotionally intense, harder to talk about, and more exposing for the client to bring up. It is less likely a client will talk about them with an organizer, but it does sometimes happen. Some of those beliefs are:

- I need to surround myself with possessions because doing so makes me feel safe and protected. My possessions comfort me or are a refuge from danger, threat, or harm.

- Making a decision such as deciding to discard something is taking a position, and making an obligation. Positions and obligations cannot be rescinded. I should avoid them.
- I don't want to be caught without something. (It is not so much about being out of something, but more about getting caught without it.)
- The future is unknown and to be feared. Saving for the future is how I prepare for the unknown and cope with fear.
- When I buy, collect, and find things it provides me with social contact not otherwise available.
- Discarding something is like death. It causes me grief.
- Things are predictable. People are not. That's why I treasure my possessions.
- My identity is defined by the possessions I have. Without them I would experience a loss of identity.

There is no circumstance in which it is appropriate for a professional organizer to directly or unilaterally challenge a strongly held belief or an attachment to an item that is associated with painful feelings of fear, grief, or loss.

Hoarding Defined

Currently, compulsive hoarding belongs to a more general category of mental disorders called Obsessive Compulsive Disorder (OCD). An obsession is an inappropriate, obtrusive, or excessive worry that causes anxiety or stress. Obsessions are forceful thoughts and images that get stuck in a person's mind and cannot be suppressed. People who hoard have what I call, "possession obsession." They might worry whether they have enough possessions, or fear losing their possessions, or may feel a deep duty to protect them, or any number of beliefs that rise to the level of obsession. A compulsion is a persistent impulse, action or behavior performed to relieve the anxiety and stress of the obsession. Compulsively acquiring new items and excessively saving all items is a way for people with possession obsession to reduce their anxiety.

There is a growing school of thought that maintains that hoarding should be unbundled from OCD. Dr. Gail Steketee and Dr. Frost, propose new criteria for hoarding which I have paraphrased here:

PROPOSED DIAGNOSTIC CRITERIA FOR COMPULSIVE HOARDING AND ACQUIRING

- The client accumulates a large number of possessions that clutter the active living spaces of the home, workplace or other personal surroundings and are kept in a disorganized fashion. If disorganized clutter is not present in other areas like the yard, vehicle, or office, it is only because family members, authorities or others have intervened to keep these areas uncluttered.
- The client has current or past difficulty resisting the urge to collect, buy or acquire free things that contribute to the clutter.
- The client is extremely reluctant to part with items, even those of very limited monetary value or utility.
- The accumulation of clutter or difficulty parting with items causes marked distress or interferes significantly with normal use of the home, workplace, or their personal surroundings, occupational or school functioning, or usual family and social activities.
- The clutter poses significant health or safety risks such as blocked egress, cluttered stairs, and fire hazard.

• The clutter causes significant conflict with family members, neighbors, or authorities such as work supervisors and landlords.

• The problem has persisted for at least six months and is not the result of a recent move, repairs to the home, the accumulation of many items resulting from the death of a family member, or other temporary circumstances.

• The clutter and the difficulty parting with items are not better accounted for by another mental disorder such as OCD, dementia, major depressive disorder, hallucinations about objects, paranoia, or bipolar disorder. This disturbance is not the result of the direct psychological effects of drugs.

Compulsive Acquisitions

You'll notice the clinical criteria for hoarding includes not only the inability to discard, but also the acquisition of large quantities of possessions of limited value. We all buy things we don't need on occasion to satisfy a want or whimsy. And it makes sense to buy things on sale in bulk when we can, even if we can't use that item right away. Many of us buy items slightly used at thrift stores and it's fun to go to flea markets as part of a weekend's relaxation or the thrill of a "good find."

The kind of acquisition referred to here is the type that results in significant stress or disruption of functioning. Compulsive acquisition entails buying items on impulse and without much concern about the impact of spending on the individual's or the family's finances. It involves ignoring the space these acquisitions will take up and the living space they will displace.

In addition to buying *new* stuff, acquisition can include buying used stuff at garage sales, yard sales, thrift stores and flea markets. Other sources of acquisition are free stuff from at-the-curb salvage, free catalogs, handouts at conferences, freebies from trade shows and even dumpster diving. Remember, people who hoard have a strong sense that objects have intrinsic, unappreciated value worthy of rescuing from the fate of the trash.

Sometimes the acquisitions begin a vicious cycle. Acquisitions cut off access to food in the kitchen, obfuscate clean clothes from dirty, and make finding necessary items nearly impossible. The practical solution is to acquire more food (and its packaging), more clothes, and more necessities and stuff them into the house right along with the existing clutter.

This book focuses more on the compulsive saving side rather than the compulsive acquiring side of the hoarding equation. The reason is that even though both excessive acquiring and excessive saving contribute to disorganization, by and large, organizers are not called upon as heavily to contend with the client's compulsion to acquire as with the ramifications of their saving. I recommend *Buried in Treasures*, pages 123-133 for excellent information on compulsive acquisitions. Sources of information about compulsive shopping are in the **Resources** section of this book.

A Word About Collecting Versus Hoarding

People who hoard collect all kinds of things — empty boxes, used greetings cards, books, and mugs are examples. They also collect *reasons* for collecting these things in abundance; all kinds of reasons that sound ironclad like frugality, environmentalism, sentimentality or knowledge.

But just because someone has a lot of one type of object and has a reason for doing so, doesn't mean it's a collection. If the client you are working with has the tendencies listed below, they are crossing the line between collector and hoarder.

* Objects are common disposables
* Objects are bought compulsively using money meant for necessities
* Purchasing the objects causes debt
* Other people cannot view or touch the objects
* Objects may be displayed but are dirty or dusty
* Objects overrun space needed for more important functions like eating or relaxing
* Finding, purchasing, and storing objects displaces time for more important functions like working or resting

There are two other hoarding behaviors that occur frequently, and particularly impact the ability of a compulsive hoarder to get and stay organized: *ambivalence* and *insight.*

Ambivalence

People who hoard are compelled to acquire and save excessively. And yet, at the same time, they often long to share their home with family and friends. Mostly, they want to set a better role model for their children or grandchildren. A house that looks nice and is welcoming is a common desire. Some hoarders, though not all, can't stand the way they live. They both want and do not want to change. It is a phenomenon called "ambivalence."

Change is difficult for everyone and we all experience conflict when we have to give up what we are used to and do something different.

Examples of ambivalence organizers encounter with hoarding clients are:

- Discarding something and then retrieving it out of the trash
- Making appointments and then breaking them
- Engaging in actions (i.e. like checking emails, answering the phone) unrelated to organizing during the organizing appointment
- Backsliding with no desire to discuss why
- Blaming events and other people

Difficult as ambivalence may be for an organizer, it is more difficult for your client. Because your client cannot consistently control their beliefs and emotional attachments to their possessions, the commitment and inability to follow through on the desire to have a less cluttered home, causes pain in the lives of compulsive hoarders.

Insight

Poor insight refers to being unable to recognize that clutter, acquisition or difficulty parting with items is excessive or unreasonable. It is not, of course, an inability to see in the visual sense. Nor is it a break with reality in the way psychoses are. I asked my client Mary Beth, "How do you explain that your apartment looks like this and your friends' apartments do not?" She responded, "I have in my house what I need. Maybe they don't want or need the things I do." On some level Mary Beth is correct. People do differ in their needs and wants.

But Mary Beth is missing the bigger point. She has to turn sideways to get into her bathroom because of the clutter. Mary Beth does not acknowledge that her clutter is excessive, nor does it seem to bother her. Lack of insight is one of the things that drive family members (and organizers) crazy. They wonder, "She's so smart. Doesn't she *see* this? If she could *see* it, surely she would do something about it." A person motivated to do something about their hoarding may also suddenly lose that insight, that glimmer that something is wrong, as soon as they have to throw something away. Insight is a fragile thing.

What Causes Hoarding?

The brain is implicated in part of the explanation for hoarding, specifically the chemical neurotransmitters dopamine and serotonin. Dopamine helps to regulate motor movements, emotions and moods and is proven to play a role in the incidence of OCD. Serotonin is also an influence on OCD. Since OCD and hoarding are correlated, both of these chemicals correlate with hoarding too. How the surplus or deficit of these neurotransmitters impact hoarding is the subject of more research. "Lower glucose metabolism in the cingulated gyros" (got that?) seems at play. "Low dorsal and anterior cingulated cortex activity" also has a role.

Interestingly, part of the reason for hoarding is that discarding may actually be experienced as punishing. Dr. Tolin and his colleagues have found that decisions to discard personal possessions activate regions in the brain associated with processing punishing or unpleasant events, and "…refusal to discard personal possessions activates regions associated with categorizing…." That means "…decisions to discard may be experienced as punishing and thus to be avoided…."

We are a society that looks for simple explanations—a particular gene, a cause and effect relationship, or something in our upbringing. We take comfort in assigning blame or being able to label a cause for a problem.

But we humans are just too complicated for a simple explanation of hoarding. Even the brain is not reducible to an organ that simply sits in our skull waiting to be scanned and measured. There is a hugely complicated system of chemicals, circuitry and electricity (to say nothing of the mind, which is different than the brain) that is involved in all mental activity. Every day scientists and researchers are struggling to find the organically-based contributing causes that will no doubt inform future treatment.

Vulnerabilities

In their book, *The Treatment of Compulsive Hoarding: A Therapist's Guide*, Doctors Sketekee and Frost, discuss "areas of vulnerabilities" that may set a person with a biological predisposition to hoard into the full-blown syndrome.

Trauma and Loss

Traumatic events in a person's history can be a factor. These events might include deprivation and poverty, constantly moving from one home to another, and most significantly, loss. Many of us experience loss in our lifetime, of a parent or other significant loved one, or loss of our home or possessions. Of course, not everyone who experiences a traumatic event becomes a hoarder, so much more research into this mechanism is needed.

In a lecture by Dr. Frost at the NYC Task Force

on Hoarding in 2004, he further notes that, "...we see parents who put their children in situations that were frightening or scary. There may be some kind of childhood deprivation of some sort. One of the themes that keeps coming up is loss which seems to extend to everything. Losing a possession to them is, in many ways, like losing a close friend or family member. This theme suggests that there is something about this phenomenon in childhood."

Heredity

A person who hoards does not automatically pass this tendency onto their children. However, the vast majority of people who hoard know of other hoarders in their family tree.

Co-Morbidity

Like many other mental disorders, hoarding rarely occurs in isolation of other mental health issues, a phenomenon psychologists call co-morbidity. While it is not true that everyone with the below conditions will develop into a hoarder, it is true that a person who hoards is likely to have one of these disorders as well:

- Depression
- Obsessive-Compulsive Personality Disorder
- Social Phobia
- Attention-Deficit/Hyperactivity Disorder

Values Gone Amuck

The proverb, "Waste not, want not," can be traced back to 1772. That's 236 years of strong societal messaging that the less we waste, the less we lack in the future. Buttressed by The Great Depression, several war-time conservation campaigns, a strong tradition of salvage and repair and, more recently, recognition that some natural resources are not limitless, many of us are conscientious about not wasting stuff. This can be true even if we individually did not personally experience these events. We try to make things last until their utility, charm, beauty or usefulness wears out. Such societal and family values are normal.

People who hoard may be more susceptible to this value than others. All kinds of factors can be at play such as personal experience with loss or trauma, overly strict parental discipline about wastefulness, a terrific imagination for the re-use of everything, and a greater-than-average sense of responsibility. According to Dr. Tolin, values gone amuck may be justified in the minds of some people who hoard, like this:

"I can think of ways to reuse this item. Therefore, I am *responsible* for doing so, and if I fail to do so, I am being *wasteful.* If I am wasteful, I will be a *rotten person.* However, I am unable to actually follow through with this plan. Therefore, in order to avoid being a rotten person, I will hold onto this item."

The Organizing Side of Hoarding

Chapter Three

Lack of organizational skills is not a symptom of hoarding, but all the research on hoarding reveals that wherever there is hoarding, there is organizational chaos. Mental health professionals who treat and study people who hoard, have discovered that they have difficulty processing information and do so significantly differently than non-hoarders. Information processing skills are strongly related to organizing skills.

If you are an organizer, you'll no doubt recognize some of these skills. I am convinced that the organizing profession can learn a great deal about how to remediate organizational skills from people who are deficient in these skills. Our hoarding clients can help us educate all our clients who are challenged to get and stay organized.

As organizers and psychologists continue to

work together, the cognitive restructuring strategies taught to patients to challenge their beliefs will include strategies developed by professional organizers. Some of us may be using techniques right now in the field that would support the goals of cognitive behavioral therapy. Likewise, skill training such as how to categorize, decision-making strategies and organizing techniques will be contributions professional organizers will increasingly make to our mental health colleagues.

Sorting and Categorizing

When it comes to organizing, categories are king. Categories give us a way to put logical things together. Categories enable us to exclude items that do not logically belong. Non-hoarders can sort through even a large pile of a vast variety of stuff, and categorize clothing, from food items, from papers. A coupon from a newspaper for a food item or an apron used for cooking food might present a slight category-crossover problem, but these can be readily resolved.

A person who hoards can also certainly sort clothing from food from paper. The problem is they drill down their categories with so much specificity that instead of a few categories with a lot of items in each, they often end up with many categories with very few items in each.

True Story

Melanie and I scooped all the clutter off her dining room table and loaded it temporarily into boxes. We assembled all her glassware on the dining room table. In many lifetimes no one could possibly use the number of cups, drinking glasses, and mugs Melanie had accumulated. They amounted to 87.

I attempted to have her make three categories: mugs, drinking glasses and cups. "This mug is a collector's item. I'll just put it out of the way," Melanie said carrying the single mug into her bedroom. "These cups are plastic," she said moving them into their own group. Then she moved several out into another group, "just for the holidays."

"I remember this. It's a glass Dad bought me. See the picture of Coney Island on it with the date 1957? It's a keeper." So that glass began another group.

"Let's put Mama's cups and saucers over here," Melanie said on her way to the cupboard to find the saucers. "I'll wrap them and send them to my niece," she hollered, perched precariously atop a chair while searching the top shelf for those long-lost saucers.

26 minutes later, Melanie had 17 different groups, the integrity of which I lost track. She tossed out a mug with an inky bottom, two cups with no handles, and five drinking glasses, a hard-won 10% of the total.

"It's as if each item is so special that it can't be categorized with other items," note the authors of *Buried in Treasures*, Drs. David Tolin, Randy O. Frost, and Gail Steketee. From an organizing point of view, having lots of small categories rather than a few large ones increases the number of decisions to make, further complicating the sorting and categorizing process.

In a 2007 article entitled, "Categorization in Compulsive Hoarding," John P. Wincze, Gail Steketee and Randy Frost reveal the results of a study on categorization. On tasks sorting common household items, the three groups of compulsive hoarders, non-hoarders with OCD, and people with neither tendency did not differ on the number of piles created nor on the amount of time taken to sort. However, on a task sorting personally relevant items, hoarding participants took more time, created more piles, and reported more anxiety than non-psychiatric controls. Hoarders also took more time than the OCD group. The results support under-inclusive categorizing for people with compulsive hoarding, but the effect was largely confined to objects of personal relevance.

Decision-Making

Organizing decisions, such as what to keep, what to discard, where to put stuff and how long to keep it, challenge many of our clients. Problems with organizing decisions (and decision-making in general) are intrinsic to the hoarding syndrome. Consider this observation by Dr. Randy Frost in a recent article, entitled "The Mish Mosh":

The Mish Mosh

Difficulty organizing possessions, more than acquiring or saving, produces most of the dysfunction associated with hoarding. For reasons we are only just beginning to understand, people with this problem pile their possessions in the middle of the room with no apparent organizational scheme. At first glance, the home of a hoarder appears filled with nothing but trash.

Closer inspection reveals mixtures of important as well as worthless stuff. Mental health specialists have long assumed that hoarders save mostly worthless or worn-out things. It turns out they save everything, valuable as well as worthless items.

More than anything hoarding is a problem with organization. Difficulties with organization seem to be related to another prominent characteristic of people who hoard—difficulty making decisions. Both organizing and decision making are largely determined by the way information gets processed... hoarders display a systematic bias to attend to unusual details of an object, like the shape and color... once noticed, these details give the object value that must be considered in any decision regarding the object. That means any decision related to a possession requires more processing."

"At times indecisiveness seems due to difficulty processing all of the information needed to make a decision," concurs Dr. Tolin. But indecision "...plagues them throughout the day, in virtually everything they do. They can't decide what to wear, where to go, what to eat... even everyday decisions feel like a major ordeal. Sometimes indecisiveness is related to beliefs such as perfectionism."

Perfectionism

Professional organizers are familiar with the backfire effect of perfectionism. Some of our clients yearn to reach a perfect level of organization and in striving for it fail because nobody can reach such a standard. And so the very goal they desire, perfectionism, is the same goal that undermines them.

They become fixated in their mind that if they cannot organize perfectly, they won't do it at all. They hold onto an item because it might be the perfect gift for someone, they let items scatter throughout the house waiting for the perfect storage solutions, they hold onto a set of dishes intending to find the perfect missing piece and so on.

Perfectionism tends to stay on the intention plane and never quite graduates to action, so the clutter mounts. Most of all they wait for *the perfect time to take action* on the stuff they have accumulated whether it is to sort, store, discard, or even use. This brand of procrastination, waiting for the perfect organizing time, complicates the picture.

A person who hoards is more afraid than non-hoarders of making a wrong decision. A wrong decision might be deciding to throw something away that might/could/should later be useful. A perfect decision would be one that has none of this risk to it. All decisions have some risk. This loss of perspective is very common with people who hoard. For them, discarding stuff is wrought with anxiety and consternation.

Organizers may think that most obstacles to decision-making and perfectionism can be overcome with a great deal of assurance that the organizer will be careful to throw nothing of value away. This kind of reassurance (even if it were true, which it is often not) does not help and can make things worse.

> What is missing for people who hoard, is the balance between the gains made by making organizing decisions and living with them versus the small consequence of making a wrong organizing decision.

Irene Tobis, a former professional organizer who is now a psychologist with a specialty in hoarding notes that, "Therapists skillfully avoid reassuring the client that they will not throw anything of value away, but rather explain that the therapist or the client might make a mistake and accidentally throw away something of value. The goal is to increase the client's comfort level with taking risks so progress can be made." Reassurance that the organizing will be perfect does the client little good, an important lesson for organizers.

There is one other version of perfectionism among people who hoard: the perfectionist hoarder. Compulsive acquisition and saving is disguised by columns and columns of perfectly stacked and aligned boxes each filled with stuff, clearly labeled shoe boxes piled one on the other from ceiling to floor and scores of shopping bags neatly filled with stuff all lined up in rows like a regiment of soldiers. I've even witnessed four off-site storage units, every inch packed tight with neatly arranged clutter.

OCD is evident in the perfectionist hoarder who spends extraordinary time and effort and rituals on gathering, assembling and maintaining compulsive acquisitions and excessively saved stuff.

Prioritizing

Prioritizing can be based on several criteria such as urgency or importance. The ability to discard items depends on prioritizing them; that is, determining the relative importance of one item from another. That's where things get really fuzzy.

People who hoard have an "attentional-bias towards non-essential details." That means small details such as design or color or shape encourage the attachment to an item. When you work with hoarding clients, they tell elaborate stories about their stuff in details that do not contribute at all to the task at hand (i.e., figuring out what to discard). This tendency is called variously, overthinking, complex thinking and cognitive elaboration. Whatever the label, it robs people who hoard of the mental clarity it takes to prioritize.

A variation on the prioritizing theme is a behavior called "churning." Your client picks up an item, decides for whatever reason that they cannot decide (which is itself a default decision) and places the item on top of the stack to indicate the importance of getting back to it. The process repeats with other items until the clutter is churned but nothing discarded. An interesting twist on this, observes Dr. Tolin, is that each time the same item is encountered, its value (importance) goes up. "I've kept it so it must be important," goes the reasoning.

Memory

The study of hoarding is complex. There are exciting investigations into the neurology of the problem and it may be concluded that people who hoard have neurologically-based memory problems to a significant degree over non-hoarders. However, the current literature does not support this contention. It is clear that when it comes to memory, people who hoard lack confidence in memory capacity. Reliance on visual reminders and beliefs about remembering and recording information all play a role.

Visual/Spatial Cues

Your hoarding clients, like other people who try to cope with disorganization, will tell you part of what makes for clutter is having to keep things in view in order to remember to do something about the item or even to remember possessing it. This is no doubt true. Margaret, one of my clients, has empty shelves and dresser drawers and prefers to stack her stuff in a jumble in the middle of the room. She churns to the top of the pile stuff she might want to notice more than other stuff. The thought of putting it away "is like burying it six-feet under." Still the visibility of items to prompt memory doesn't quite explain the jumble and why it is in the middle of the room.

Dr. Christina Gilliam, a postdoctoral fellow at the Anxiety Disorders Center at the Institute for Living in Hartford, Connecticut says these visual reminders have a significant meaning spatially as well. Each item, perceived to be so unique that it can't be grouped with similar items, means that categories cannot be used to place and find things. "...categorization relies on a memory-based approach to finding items rather than a category-based approach. In other words, individuals with compulsive hoarding attempt to place and find items based on visual spatial recall (remembering where an item was last seen) instead of a categorical recall (remembering where a certain category of item is usually placed). This approach to categorizing makes the process of placing and finding items more complicated and ineffective." Imagine trying to remember where you put everything without the benefit of categories. It would tax anybody's memory.

Underestimating Memory

Leaving things in view is a time-honored memory aid. It works. Compulsive hoarders become so reliant on these visual cues and reminders, they lose confidence in their own ability to remember things. The reminders, left everywhere, lose their signal and become just a part of the overall clutter. In treatment, compulsive hoarders can regain a more realistic appraisal of their memory capacity.

Beliefs About Information

What presents itself as concern about memory sometimes ends up being mistaken beliefs about information. Your client might think that they cannot rely on their memory to keep up with facts and events and information so they keep magazines and newspapers. It is really the anxiety of keeping up, of not falling behind that motivates the excessive saving.

Perfectionism sometimes also comes into the picture in the form of wanting to perfectly record events and information. And then there is the nagging worry that perhaps there is something of real importance in one of those newspapers so to be sure, it has to be kept. I hate to even think what the impact of the unlimited access to information afforded by the Internet does to people susceptible to information hoarding.

Inattention/Distractibility

Attention is the ability to filter out distractions so we can focus on the task at hand. Organizing anything requires some degree of attention. Sometimes as in organizing a complex project, a great deal of attention is required.

You might think that sorting through clutter, especially a lot of useless stuff, would be pretty easy to attend to and even if one gets distracted, simple to return to. It turns out that compulsive hoarders have a good deal more internal and external distraction than non-hoarders.

"For people with compulsive hoarding, the distractions are more frequent, more intense, and more compelling—and often they come from inside, rather than outside the person," notes Dr.

Tolin. Internal distractions can include random thoughts, ideas, worries, mental to-do tasks, the weighing of choices, and anxiety about decisions.

Assessment

C
h
a
p
t
e
r

F
o
u
r

Organizers are not in the mental health business and do not diagnose; instead, we take a look at the environment of a client and infer from that if we have a hoarding client on our hands. When I talk about "assessing" your client I mean objectively evaluating their physical environment. We can also be very observant of quality of life clues. These are a little trickier because they can be more subjective. Together, objective measures, experience and a good dash of common sense make it clear as to whether you are working with a person who hoards.

The Clutter/Hoarding Scale©

I founded the NSGCD in 1998. Its current mission is to explore, develop, and disseminate to professional organizers and related professionals, organizing methods, approaches, and solutions that benefit chronically disorganized people. Related professionals are social workers, medical practitioners, law enforcement, teachers, learning experts, researchers, and professionals in other fields who are interested in aspects of disorganization/organization. The NSGCD is an invaluable source of education for every organizer, even an organizer who chooses not to work with chronically disorganized or hoarding clients. For more about the NSGCD and its educational offerings, certificates of study and certifications go to **www.nsgcd.org**.

In 2002, NSGCD members Heidi Schulz, Sheila Delson, Cindy Glovinsky and Terry Prince wrote the Clutter/Hoarding Scale© (CHS). Its primary purpose is to establish a standardized framework that describes the predominant features of escalating levels of clutter. The CHS evaluates four of these features or categories:

- Structure and Zoning
- Pets and Rodents
- Household Functions
- Sanitation and Cleanliness

Level I is the least severe and Level V is the most severe. You can view the CHS in its entirety in **Appendix I**. The CHS is an evolving document that may have changed since publication of this book. To be assured you are using the most accurate

The **Clutter/Hoarding Scale** gives organizers, the client, the client's family and professionals in other fields, a common language and terminology to describe household conditions and functions. You can download it at http://www.nsgcd.org/

information go to **www.nsgcd.org/resources/clutterhoardingscale.php**.

I suggest you print it out for easy reference.

Assessing escalating levels of clutter is a reliable clue to how severe hoarding is, and it has several advantages:

- Particular levels might suggest certain methods to try
- Particular levels suggest the addition of resources and services to organizing services
- Appropriate training, experience and certifications may be attendant to each level

The single most important aspect of the CHS

is that it is a *standardized* assessment tool for use by organizers, families, community agencies, social workers, clinicians, and first responders. For example, let's say a social worker makes a home visit to a client and discovers a severe hoarding situation. That social worker can call up a local professional organizer and report, "I've got a Level IV client on my hands who needs your help." The local professional organizer will immediately know what the situation is. Or, a professional organizer can call a social worker and say "I've got a Level IV client who needs assistance," and the social worker will know what that means. Of course, the CHS is not yet familiar to all the social workers in the U.S but someday it will be the standard by which hoarding is assessed across a wide range of disciplines. The CHS goes a long way in promoting cross-discipline collaboration on the very complex problem of hoarding.

No single photograph can ever depict the complete image of a client's CHS level. I've included photos to help you get a feel for the escalation of clutter indicating increasing severity of hoarding. Please note that the CHS itself does not use photographs.

Level I – Holly's house is structurally sound and the front and back doorways are accessible. She can climb up and down the stairway fairly easily. As housekeeping standards go, she lets things slide. The trash tends to overflow before she gets to it but the house doesn't smell. She has a dog and a cat that have an occasional "accident."

Paper clutter covers all the surfaces like tables, furniture and the floor in small stacks. Holly has two secret rooms stuffed to the gills with an assortment of stuff. The pantry,

attic, closets, cupboards and shelves are crowded and one gets the feeling the house has just about hit its maximum. It is all she can do to keep the living room clear enough for the family to watch TV and relax.

Is a Level I on the CHS scale a compulsive hoarder? It is not stated in the CHS where the actual compulsive hoarder is on the scale. That's because the clinical definition of a compulsive hoarder and the CHS are not calibrated together. So, I can't really tell you if Holly is a compulsive hoarder, but I can tell you that without some assistance she will devolve into Level II on the CHS. The Level I and Level II client reaches out to a professional organizer because they are concerned that things are starting on a downward trend they find difficult or impossible to reverse. Their distress and the disruption caused by the clutter, is enough to spend precious time and money on.

Level II - Harvey would not be able to exit his house if there was a fire, nor would the fire department find it easy to gain entry. His doorways are blocked by clutter and they barely open. He has to step over clutter to enter any room in his house. A good deal of the clutter is not useful or worth keeping. The part that is, simply isn't put away.

The living room resembles a big storage area with clothes and other clutter making it very difficult to find a place to sit. His air conditioner is on the fritz and the dishwasher doesn't drain. His dog and cat are definitely generating odors and dander. The trash in the kitchen is overwhelming the trash can and it looks like it has been there for weeks.

Level III – Arlene can't use her kitchen for anything other than an occasional drink of water. Only the toilet and sink in the bathroom are accessible. She sleeps on a bed surrounded by clutter. The mix of useful to useless items tilts substantially toward the latter with clutter turning most of her living spaces into clutter storage areas, including the tub.

The level of sanitation is so poor that, if further neglected, health hazards such as rodent or insect infestation, mold, mildew, and contaminated food preparation surfaces are inevitable. The place smells. Food is spoiling. The hot water does not get hot and the ice cubes do not freeze. The front porch steps are broken. There is a roof leak somewhere, observable by the water stain on the ceiling. Outside, the wooden lawn furniture is decayed, boxes cram the porch, and Arlene's car is parked on the street because the garage is maxed out.

Level IV – Robin is in a bad way. The structural damage to his house has been neglected for over six months. There are cracks from the ceiling to the floor, the gutters are gone, a window is boarded up with plywood, and it is clear from the odor that the plumbing is not working as it should in the bathroom. Clutter is heaped in a long mound from the front door to the back of the house, shoulder high in all directions. Trash is piled high and evident on the floor. There are no clean dishes or utensils.

Robin sleeps on the couch in a sleeping bag to avoid bed bugs. He brings in his meals and eats them off a small tray in front of a large TV set from a cozy chair. This small area where he eats and watches TV is like a little cocoon. Paint and cleaning fluids are visible in cans in the hall.

Only an expert can tell if the droppings in the house belong to mice, rats, or squirrels. Robin has three cats and two dogs exceeding the Humane Society limit of 4 animals for living quarters his size. He stores newspapers in the oven (which he does not use, but where they remain a fire hazard because they are flammable.) The odor is noxious to the uninitiated.

Level V – Believe it or not, there is a level above Robin's. Basic utilities such as water, heat, sewer and electricity are lacking entirely or very insufficient.

Hazards such as standing water or faulty wiring are obvious. The presence of rodents and insects is visible and pervasive. The bathroom and kitchen are inaccessible and inoperative.

This is the home of a squalor hoarder. It is rare. And it is even more unlikely that such an individual will seek your services. It requires money, effort, motivation and a state of mind that makes it unlikely as a self-referred client. However, you may be referred such a client under more coercive conditions from an agency, conservator, trustee, court or other source.

The priority at every level is to address the safety and health hazards first.

There is a level of self-neglect and squalor that may be above a Level V. This individual is the province of governmental or private agencies whose job it is to protect people who cannot make sound judgments and are a danger to their own welfare. Henriette Kellum, a licensed clinical social worker with 28 years of service in public agencies would call in her "gang busters" for these situations. "We're talking here about people living among dead animals, feces, blocked sewage, in imminent danger of the house falling in on itself, fire hazards…that kind of thing. With a court order in hand, the person can be legally removed." In these circumstances a co-morbid condition like depression or dementia or psychoses of one kind or another is almost certainly present. Their capacity to make sound judgments is impaired as indicated by the level of self-neglect. You cannot enter into contracts or agreements with a person whose judgment is impaired so if you participate in a hoarding project, be certain the conservator or trustee is the responsible party when it comes to paying your bills, signing agreements, establishing communication, etc.

Red Flags, Stop Signs and Exit Strategies

Sometimes you simply cannot go through with a client situation no matter how skillful and experienced you are because the situation is too unsafe, unhealthy or untenable. On the other hand, you cannot assume that just because a person is a hoarder that you are necessarily in any more danger than with other clients. The guru on personal safety is Debbie Stanley, a professional organizer who is also a trained counselor and a leading member of the NSGCD. You can purchase

If you are "first on the scene" in a Level V home and there is imminent threat or danger to the individual, do the right thing. Call an agency with a mission to help people such as the United Way or call the Sheriff's Department if you don't know a specific governmental agency that can help.

her conference tapes on personal safety at **www.napo.org.** If you are going somewhere you've never before been or plan to be away for hours, tell someone where you are going, and keep your cell phone with you. That's just general good practice for all organizers.

True Story

I can recall one time when I was "first on the scene." John's neighbors, who lived a mile from his rural community, suspected him of being a hoarder because of the extent of stuff out on the lawn, porch and in the driveway. John is 67 and he has no relatives and since he was retired and kept to himself, his situation did not come to the attention of any authorities. He was pretty self-sufficient and didn't need to call upon public assistance of any type. Out of the blue, John called me. I was the first person in his home in 17 years.

The State of Georgia was building a highway right through John's property. He had to let the assessor in to make an offer on the property and then he had to move out quickly. It was very troubling to me to have to report John to the Department of Aging, an agency I knew had resources for people John's age.

There was no way he could afford my services. He was unable to cope with even the simplest of discarding decisions. And he was overwhelmed with finding another home, packing up his possessions, leaving the trash behind and dealing with the wrecking ball looming in his immediate future.

I had no choice, ethically, even though he was opposed to my doing so. It was awful to know he was angry with me. But that weighed less on my conscience than his being homeless.

Exit Strategies

You don't a need logical, well-thought out

reason or explanation to exit any client situation that feels unsafe or out of control, whether it is a hoarding client or not. Trust your intuition. Simply LEAVE, even if you have to make up an excuse. Your safety is primary over customer relations, loyalty, money or any other competing feeling. I have had only two clients in 20 years who posed a safety concern for me and I "fired" them. That's how rare it is.

Here are the two exit strategies I've used:

"I'm sorry. I made a mistake. This job is outside of my training. I'm going."

The person was very hostile (bearing out my suspicion of their instability) and kept wanting an explanation. I just repeated the same phrase over and over until I got into my car.

"My phone just vibrated. I have a family emergency. I'm leaving now."

This person felt like a threat to my safety, so I made up this excuse and left.

Of course, if there is no safety issue and you simply find yourself in over your head, the client situation turned out to be different than you thought or you really don't know how to help the client, be as supportive as you can in exiting the situation. I'm comfortable saying, "This is not the kind of work I do. May I refer you to another organizer who is a better fit?" Or, "This job calls for a specialist. May I refer you to someone with specialized experience in this area?" A referral to another organizer can be made either by giving your client their contact information or by asking the referred organizer to contact your client with your client's permission. Ask which your client prefers.

Red Flags

Rarely, but on occasion, one of the issues on the next page may arise with a client (hoarding or non-hoarding). If you observe these red flags, discuss the client with a qualified mental health professional available through the National Study Group on Chronic Disorganization at **www.nsgcd.org** or with a trusted therapist in your area.

* Reclusive to the extent the person does not go outdoors

- Baby talk
- Overly fearful of germs
- Crying often or uncontrollably
- Talk of suicide
- Not arising from their bed
- Animal Hoarding

True Story

A woman called me and described herself "like the lady on Oprah," so immediately I knew she was a person who hoards. What I didn't know was that the woman had not permitted anyone to enter her apartment for over seven years.

After I arrived at her home, I waited on the sidewalk while the woman lowered a bucket down to me on a rope with a bell on it. The bucket had photographs of the interior of the apartment. From her window, the woman yelled down, "Nice meeting you. Can you write down three things I should do to have less clutter? There's a pad and pencil in the bucket." I looked over the photos and wrote back "Let me study these and I'll get back to you."

I asked a neighbor passing by about the

woman whom she described as a "shut-in." "A neighborhood kid buys her food using the bucket. She sends down a bag of garbage once a day. She has an air conditioner going in the summer and waves to us that she is alright on cold days," the neighbor reported.

I spoke with the landlord who said her rent is paid up and though she never comes out she seems in a good mood. The photographs revealed newspapers, magazines, and papers stacked almost to the ceiling but no clear evidence of food or fecal refuse. Of course, without pictures of the kitchen, I couldn't be sure.

Though the woman was completely socially isolated, I felt she was not in imminent danger. The local police were aware of her situation. Neighbors were keeping an eye out for her safety. I returned to the rope and rang the bell. Down came the bucket. My note to her read:

Three Steps to Less Clutter

#1   Gravity will injure you soon. Eliminate 3 feet of newspapers and replace it with fresh newspapers

#2 Be certain your bell, bucket and rope stay in excellent shape

#3 Have a nice day.

The woman waved, I waved back and walked away from the job. It was clear she wouldn't let me in and I couldn't see her lowering clutter down bucket by bucket after all these years, so I moved on.

A Word About Animal Hoarding

We've all read the stories about people with scores of cats and dogs in their homes, some dead, some alive, most ill. Even small towns have their "cat lady."

Hoarding animals can cause disease, vermin, insect infestation and other health hazards to you and to the owner of the animal. Let the authorities trained in animal hoarding deal with these situations. The animals can suffer from starvation, disease, and anti-social behavior like biting and scratching because of the cramped quarters. Feces and the decomposing of the remains of dead animals are also sometimes evident.

Animal hoarding, though on the rise, is very

rare among compulsive hoarders. It may be associated with any number of mental disorders. A discussion of animal hoarding is beyond the scope of this book, but you can find helpful information on the topic in the **Resources** section of this book.

Assessing Yourself

Working with hoarding clients is new territory for the organizing profession. We are learning a great deal about how hoarding is distinguished from chronic disorganization in general, and what array of resources seems to hold the most promise for sustained results. We are also learning more and more about the specific education, training, experience, and certifications that enable organizers to transfer organizing skills to these individuals, and be part of a broader solution to end their hoarding behaviors. Your best source for this information about education and training is the NSGCD. Always check their website for the most current information.

Currently, the NSGCD advises: "No special

knowledge in working with the chronically disorganized is necessary for Level I. A Level II household requires additional knowledge and understanding of chronic disorganization. A Level III household requires significant training in chronic disorganization. Recommended guidelines for Level III and above households are being developed."

The NSGCD offers a rigorous course of study that culminates in a Certificate of Study in Basic Hoarding Issues. I am pursuing this certificate.

To obtain it you must first earn a Certificate in Study in Chronic Disorganization. The details for both certifications can be found at **www.nsgcd.org.** Future NSGCD guidelines will further clarify the relationship between chronic disorganization and hoarding. They will also include recommendations for managing hoarding projects, collaborative therapy recommendations, guidelines for complying with government agency regulations and reporting, and specific organizing techniques.

If you are a newer organizer or an organizer beginning to see hoarding clients, I'd like to offer you a set of serious questions to ask yourself. They'll help you discover if working with clients who hoard is for you. These questions are inspired by Kristin Bergfeld's teleclass presentation to the NSGCD in 2008. Since 1987, her company, Bergfeld's Estate Clearance Service has been managing estate projects, downsizing people's homes when they move to assisted living, and helping clients whose hoarding patterns have put them at risk. Ask yourself the following questions to clarify whether working with hoarding clients is for you (or not!)

Are You Someone Who Can Work With People Who Hoard?

Am I good at managing within chaos? Lots of clutter usually results in a lot of chaos. There likely are no storage, shelves, cabinets or closets to put things away. Clear, flat surfaces are rare. It may be difficult to decide where to start. Several people and interested parties are usually involved with you on a project. Addressing your client's emotional issues can be especially challenging as you go along. Your usual feeling of competence (and confidence!) can be shaken.

Can I be more than just a rescuer? Professional organizers are 'people-people' and natural nurturers. Because you are empathetic, hard working and creative, you may mistakenly think you can rescue every client from a bad situation. A client who hoards "saves" herself with hard work, commitment and openness to change. It's not about you.

Can I tolerate poor working conditions? Usually, homes of people who hoard are dusty and have offending odors and varying types of infestation. Some homes can be sites of squalor and grime with poor light and ventilation. Your movement in and around the home will be restricted. How well do you function in such a work environment?

Do I have the stamina? De-cluttering is stressful physical work requiring lifting, bending, maneuvering around piles of possessions and stretching for what can be hours on end. Simultaneously, you will need to oversee all aspects of the project including others on the team and monitor your client. Even though you take breaks, it can be a long, hard day.

Am I patient? Organizers are quick thinkers and problem-solvers. Some clients who hoard may not be. Guiding clients through the decisions about letting go of their stuff requires great patience. The progress is not something the organizer can control. How well can you tolerate the pace of a hoarding project?

Am I understanding and non-judgmental? Remember, in addition to being non-judgmental in what you say, you have to be attentive to your body language and facial expressions. It is important to process your own reactions and not to convey your frustration to, nor to offend the client.

Can I manage my allergies? Don't put yourself at risk if you are highly-allergic to dust, mold, mildew, dust or pet dander unless you are certain you can manage your allergies with protective gear, and, if needed, medication.

Am I a team player? On complex projects, you have service providers, other organizers, and probably more than one person to answer to in addition to your client. It takes a lot of skill to work with others effectively intensively.

Am I willing to read leases, court orders, citations, ordinances, codes, or other documents with legal language? Nobody is asking for you to be an attorney. But, it's important that you are aware of documents and citations that you will encounter in your work. Your eyes shouldn't glaze over at just the thought at reviewing common legal documents that may be relevant to the situation.

The Team Approach to Hoarding Projects

Chapter Five

Returning a home to functionality and giving living space back to a family is a great gift. If you ever watched Peter Walsh, the creator of the television program *Clean Sweep,* on the Oprah Show, you saw he is a very skillful organizer and talented at counseling and coaching people through emotional glitches during complex hoarding projects. His clients give testimony to the therapeutic effects of a thorough-going de-cluttering project, even without formal therapy or on-going maintenance. A unique organizer and a unique client can occasionally make huge progress that is sustained over time. I've seen it happen more than once. Or a client will not be quite so severely disabled by hoarding that they can make significant change and with intense maintenance, keep up the good work.

Given what we know about how hard it is for people who hoard to change how they think and behave, the overwhelming clutter they face and the organizational challenges they face, for more reliable, reproducible results, a team approach to hoarding is best.

In a perfect world, the hoarding project you undertake will have the complete cooperation of your client. A mental health practitioner who understands hoarding would be on your team and make on-site visits and provide affordable in-office sessions. The family would be non-judgmental, compassionate and available to help with recycling, cleaning and all sorts of errands. The governmental agencies in your town would be familiar with hoarding and provide temporary housing, storage, dumpsters, haz-mat suits, masks, shovels and other equipment and supplies.

You would be well-trained and certified as a professional organizer with a hoarding specialization. Your client would have a budget big enough to hire you and your team of organizers. In a matter of days the house would be de-cluttered, cleaned and returned to functional order. Your client's possessions, carefully removed from the premises would be returned and organized. Your client would have on-going cleaning services and other kinds of assistance. Your client's hoarding issues would be appropriately engaged and she would be on the road to recovery.

The truth is this "dream team" is just that, a dream. To give you an idea what it really takes, consider the hoarding project aired on The Oprah Show. It took 100 people eight weeks and 2500 "man-hours". If the client was charged directly, the project would exceed over $100,000.00. Clearly, flexibility and resourcefulness are needed to produce good results. Not every client can afford therapy and organizing and support services. Not every organizer has the skill to assemble and manage such a team. And not every locality has the resources, talent, interest, or funds to press into service for your clients. But with creativity and hard work you can make smart modifications that will benefit your client.

A team approach combines specially trained

professional organizers, some version of appropriate mental health care, supplemental services (i.e., super-duper house cleaning service) and family support. I know what you're thinking. If we're organizers and not in the mental health business, aren't we diagnosing when we suggest to a client they might need care that is out of our training? Actually: no. It is not diagnosing when you counsel a client that they would benefit from therapy, any more so than when a family member suspects depression and suggests therapy, or a teacher sees learning problems and recommends an evaluation. Counseling people to seek help with problems that injure their quality of life or undermine their daily functioning is not diagnosing. It matters a lot how and when it is said, something that will be covered soon.

Why Do You Need a Therapist On Your Team?

Experienced professional organizers report that on occasion a client who finds getting organized particularly challenging, will sometimes cry out of shame, or be terribly embarrassed by the

way their home looks. They may express nervous-
ness about organizing because it is not something
they do well, or they might do it wrong, or they
simply fear changing the familiar way they are
used to seeing and doing things. Though an
organizer can be taken aback by these emotions on
the job, managing them is not usually difficult. A
gentle word of encouragement, a break, or a brief
conversation can clear the air. Sometimes just
giving air to a concern or problem can help resolve
it.

You can learn to engage in conversations with
clients that help challenge their assumptions about
why they acquire things, why they keep them and
for how long. You can learn to guide them to
express conflict or doubt. And we can learn how to
coach a client through obstacles so they can better
align their lives with their stated goals. But you
cannot undo a hardwired compulsion or a deep set
emotional attachment. That's the role of therapy.

True Story

Doug, a hoarding client of mine, and I spent
several hours sorting one paper at a time in

an apartment so filled with papers we needed to turn sideways to move about. He agonized over each piece of paper, fearing that if he threw it away it would be needed later and not replaceable. After three painfully slow hours, Dave generated one trash bag of paper for discard.

Two days later, at 4 in the morning, Dave called me at home asking if I knew where the dog food coupon for 30¢ off was. I told him it was inappropriate for him to call me at home for any reason. He reacted angrily. Then he cried and said he wanted to continue organizing with me.

If Doug were in therapy he would have a safe and unthreatening place to talk about the significance of this dog food coupon incident and his underlying beliefs and feelings. Cognitive-behavioral therapy would teach him skills to engage and change his thinking which would modify his behaviors. As his organizer, I could help support those skills and we could bring up his distress in therapy together. Instead, I had to fire him as a client.

Another reason therapy can be important is

that it is a useful context for family members to have an honest but non-abusive way of talking to the person who hoards and expressing their feelings about how the hoarding has hurt them. Hoarding takes its toll on everyone in the family. Indeed, it is not uncommon for family members to seek therapy before the individual who hoards does.

And, finally, therapy is also a way for people who hoard to get support for other conditions that commonly co-exist with hoarding. These are called co-morbid conditions. The most common ones are OCD, OC-PD, depression, social anxiety, AD/HD, bi-polar disorder and social phobia.

Cognitive-behavioral therapy (CBT) has proven to be the most effective kind of therapy for people who hoard. CBT is based on the concept that our *thoughts* cause our feelings and behaviors instead of just external things like events or other people or situations. The premise of CBT is if we can change the way we think (cognition), we can change the way we feel and act. It differs from traditional "talk" psychotherapy in that it is action-oriented and solution-focused.

The individual and therapist learn to sort, let go, and control acquisition compulsions through various exercises and assignments, depending on the person's fears, beliefs and needs. The result is a structured way of confronting, challenging and changing behavior.

It is very hard work and takes time but unlike traditional psychotherapy, it is limited to the time it takes to reach goals and objectives the client and the therapist design together. "We are studying the effects of CBT for people with compulsive hoarding, and our early evidence suggests the majority of people show substantial improvements in the level of clutter and how they feel", reports Dr. Tolin. Few people are "cured" however, in the sense of having no clutter and no problem ever again dealing with it. Most improve, have more clutter than average and have to keep at it to stay under control.

Introducing Clients to Therapy

It's easiest to introduce a client to therapy

when it is normalized, that is, when it is simply a part of your model for doing hoarding project. Remember Janette, the professional organizer in the first chapter? We left her in the midst of a large-scale hoarding project with Hope, worried she may be giving Hope false hope (sorry about that) and dreading the painfully slow, drudgery of the project. With a therapist on Hope's team, Janette might have left Hope with this message:

> "You are in luck, Hope. I've got a very effective approach to excessive saving. It is a team approach. On the team is a top, notch professional organizer trained in working with people who excessively save. We'll do a few organizing sessions together first.

> This is very hard work and often emotional and I want to be sure the organizing "sticks" so your money is well spent. I have a hand-picked therapist. She makes house calls! She'll come by to talk to you. That way the therapist, you and I can come up with the best strategies for you to stop the clutter. It's all done in strict confidence.

> The team also includes services when we need them, like a super-duper

housecleaning service and a repairman, who won't judge you and it is all confidential. I even have a few jobs your family or friends can do to help if we decide that's okay."

Another organizer who works with hoarding clients shared her approach with me. She says, "There is so much going on here: the clutter, the way you feel about your stuff, trying to change… it's overwhelming. I'd like you to have all the support you can possibly have. May I invite a therapist to visit with you here in your home? She can help us 'get to the bottom' of the problem emotionally and physically. It's confidential."

With clients whose hoarding is not quite so severe, therapy can be introduced as a preventive tactic. After a few organizing sessions when trust has been gained and they are reassured about confidentiality, I say something like:

"We're really making progress. I want to be sure this progress "sticks". It is extremely effective with excessive saving for a therapist to visit once or twice and talk to you because underneath the clutter are emotional issues. I want to be sure your money is well spent. I have a hand-picked therapist. She makes house calls! With her help, you and I can learn strategies to help stop the clutter from coming back. It's all done in strict confidence."

I don't mention anything about on-going therapy, office visit therapy or anything other than the therapist visiting on-site once or twice. I figure it's the therapist's role to encourage longer-term therapy which is part of why I have selected her to collaborate with. She is in a much better position than I to recommend longer-term therapy. If you pursue training through the NSGCD in working with individuals who hoard, you'll learn other techniques for maximizing the mental health care of your clients.

Entering therapy, however, briefly, carries with it stigma. Stigma is one of the reasons people don't seek mental health care. Assure your client the knowledge that your client is in therapy, or even has been referred to therapy, is strictly confidential and is not information shared with others.

I am under no delusion that every client will

take advantage of therapy even if qualified therapists are available. Therapy may be too expensive for your client. Perhaps they cannot be convinced of the value, or they want to avoid the stigma. Some organizers make therapy conditional on the delivery of de-cluttering and organizing services. I do not. However, if a hoarding client above Level II declines therapy, I take a few extra measures:

- Encourage them again later on in the process
- Adjust my client's expectations about sustained, long-term results
- Give them a free self-help book
- Leave a list of support groups and other resources
- Leave a business card of a OCD/CBT therapist in case they change their mind

Therapeutic Options

To locate a therapist with CBT training, and a OCD background specializing in hoarding, go to:

- The Obsessive Compulsive Foundation website for a list of providers by state (**www.ocfoundation.org**)

- The National Association of Cognitive Behavioral Therapists at **www.nacbt.org** and locate a hoarding specialist
- Contact your state mental health association for a referral

On the one hand, it is not easy to find a therapist with specific training in hoarding. On the other hand, just any old therapist will not do. On the other hand, maybe some therapy is better than no therapy. On the other hand…. well, I think you get the idea. I cannot tell you what to do if a CBT specifically trained in hoarding is not available to you when you have a hoarding client. Discuss your specific situation with a professional organizer certified in a hoarding specialty, or with a mental health professional associated with the NSGCD to explore alternative therapeutic options.

- Consider an OCD therapist with CBT training even if they are not hoarding specialists
- Determine if there is a therapist-led OCD or hoarding support group available in your area
- Check with your local university medical center or teaching hospital for a psychiatric in-patient or outpatient OCD or anxiety disorder clinic.

- Team up with a hoarding specialist therapist by phone
- Team up with a professional organizer who is also a therapist

Collaborative Therapy for Clutter Management©

A full-fledged team approach, called Collaborative Therapy for Clutter Management (CT) was created by Heidi Schulz, CPO-CD® a professional organizer specializing in working with compulsive hoarders and Roland Rotz, Ph.D., a clinical psychologist specializing in overcoming environmental and emotional clutter. Here is a detailed overview of that approach:

At its core CT involves the client working side by side with any combination of organizers, therapists, counselors, coaches, family, and community service agencies. Together, the team facilitates interventions that help create and maintain environmental change in the home, as well as lasting therapeutic change within the client. Using a blend of Motivational Interviewing and Cognitive-Behavioral Therapy, CT helps clients identify and reframe the emotional and physical connections to their "stuff" in order to develop corrective alternatives for long-term solutions. On site, qualified and experienced organizers can provide keen observations to the reality of clutter and acquisitions in the hoarding environment.

As Schulz explains, "An organizer is often the first person to enter a hoarder's home in decades. We experience the odors, darkness, the sheer volume and oppression of 'stuff'."

Collaborating team members, such as a therapist specializing in Obsessive- Compulsive Disorder and Cognitive-Behavioral Therapy or community service agencies may be called to the home to assess and evaluate the health and safety risks to the hoarder. As part of the team, organizers can avoid the isolation, frustration, client backsliding, burnout and re-accumulation of clutter that is so common in the typical cyclical nature of clutter that we know all too well.

Any combination of other support personnel may be involved such as: family, friends, organizational assistants, animal control, building safety and code enforcement, adult protective services and restoration/cleaning services.

"The unaware therapist working with a compulsive hoarder and acquirer may never get an accurate picture of the clutter/hoarding situation for a variety of reasons. Frequently the clients presenting complaint is about the emotional complications of the clutter/hoarding situation without ever disclosing their physical environment. If the client feels shame and embarrassment about their living condition, they fear that sharing this information will lead to the sudden removal of collected items to which they feel extremely attached. In contrast, some clients show little insight about the health and safety risks of hoarding while freely discussing the volume of material as if it represents a bubble of safety surrounding them," observes Dr. Rotz.

The CT model involves creating written agreements between all parties. For example, some details might include collective decisions to remove only those items to which the client has previously agreed. Other significant concerns involve items that may represent conflicted or traumatized aspects of the client's life to which they feel extremely attached, called 'traumatized attachments.' Therapeutic intervention may be required before decisions are made about these conflicted items. Once the decisions have been made, agreements can be written up, signed, dated by all concerned and posted in a prominent location so that they can be referred to as needed. Collaborative Therapy for Clutter Management© is a supportive, flexible and evolving protocol that we have found to be effective in assisting our compulsive hoarding and acquiring clients.

The preceding description is reprinted with permission of Heidi Schulz, CPO-CD® and Roland Rotz, Ph.D.

CT in Action – Lynn and Mo

Lynn Mino, CPO-CD® Professional Organizer and Mo Osburne, RN, CPO-CD® who work together in Virginia, have a large network of therapists who refer clients to them. As a nurse, Mo is active with a women's health networking group. They speak at networking events of social workers, psychotherapists, geriatric care managers, psychiatrists and other health related professionals about hoarding and their collaborative model. The Fire Marshal referred a Level V person to Lynn and Mo with a deadline to correct a list of code violations (blocked entrances and exits, combustibles too close to fire sources, blocked air vents, etc.) **in 10 days!** Lynn and Mo met with the client, who, as you can imagine is very motivated since the consequence of non-compliance might be the loss of abode or large fines or both. They collaborated together to create a plan to address the code violations. In this proposal, it is clarified that the individual, and not the Fire Marshal or county or some other party was the client and responsible for paying the costs, all detailed in the proposal the client signs. Lynn and Mo have their own supplies and equipment but if they needed something additional, it would be in the proposal. (See **Appendix III** for a list of recommended supplies and equipment.)

They report to the Fire Marshal regularly on their progress and he is allowed to view the progress first-hand. The client is referred to an appropriate therapist from the connections Lynn and Mo have made doing networking in that community. The client and the therapist have an agreement, and Lynn and Mo and the client have an agreement. For this client private cleaning companies, debris removal, pest control, haulers and appraisers were utilized. Agreements with the client to enter the premises in their absence and stipulating that they have home owners insurance are also signed. (Samples of these agreements are in **Appendix II**.)

Lynn and Mo sat with the client's attorney as advocates for the client at a hearing in front of a hoarding task force. In some jurisdictions, a hoarding task force can have a say in whether a person who hoards can remain in their home and under what conditions. "Another important reason for your client to consent to therapy is that it gives us, the organizer, more leverage with the hoarding task force, the fire marshal, the courts or other authorities that the client is committed to turning things around. We can then buy the client more time to meet everyone's objectives. " On occasion, Lynn and Mo will have a client who is self-referred. Lynn notes, "There is less of a sense of urgency with a self-referred client and the progress can be painfully slow." Still, they prevail.

CT in Action – Randi Lyman

In "Building Relationships with Your Core Collaborative Team", Randi B. Lyman, CPO-CD® gives great advice on finding therapists based on her experience relocating from Illinois to Austin, Texas. She writes:

I was on a mission. I wanted to meet psychotherapists who practiced cognitive behavioral therapy and worked in the field of obsessive compulsive disorders, specifically with hoarders. I also wanted to meet psychotherapists specialized in ADHD.

I researched psychiatric providers online and used the old-fashioned method, the phone book. Once I had a list of names, I made calls and set up meetings to introduce myself, explain how I could work with them and their patients, and begin to build a referral base for my clients. I built on my prior experience in Illinois, attaining positive results by creating a core collaborative team. It is easier to meet professionals if you have something to offer them whether that is information, successes from past clients, plans to create programs, or systems therapists will find beneficial to their clients/ patients.

In Austin, psychological teams rent office space together. I hosted a 'lunch and learn' and through hard work, met eight therapists in two months, including a therapist that runs the local OCD Clinic. He told me about an OCD support group and I was invited to sit in. The group leader was a great resource for me. She referred me to a lot of people with hoarders in their families. I started working with these individuals and their families. My website also drives therapists and psychiatrists my way. *But I have found the very best way to create a relationship with a therapist is through your clients who already have an established relationship with a therapist.* I have been very successful in working with the therapists of my clients. This 'warm lead' is beneficial in getting through barriers and getting to know therapists we can work with.

In one instance, after a brief time of working with a client, we both started to feel frustrated by lack of progress. We were moving items from one room to the next, getting nowhere. If we did discard an item, she would go on a dumpster-diving expedition after I left. She was resistant to change, frozen in fear and I realized to get anywhere I needed some professional guidance. She said she felt frustrated and annoyed with herself because it was so difficult for her to make decisions since she felt extremely attached to her possessions. She was already in therapy. I asked her for permission to speak to her therapist. She thought this was a good idea and discussed it with her therapist. The therapist agreed and scheduled a meeting for the three of us in her office.

My client signed a consent form with her therapist to give her permission to talk to me about the client's compulsive hoarding issues and psychological disorders that directly contributed to her hoarding behavior. My client and the therapist signed a 'Client's

Right to Privacy' contract to protect her privacy rights. Only psychological issues pertinent to our organizing work were disclosed. We created these guidelines upfront, establishing clear boundaries for our work together, and determined how we would communicate with each other.

In the session, I discussed what we had done in the client's home to date and the client's goals for each organizing session. The client shared her perspective on our work together and explained her frustration with herself because the de-cluttering process was so difficult for her. Prior to my working with this client, the therapist had been to her home a few times and understood her living situation. I showed the therapist 'before' pictures of my client's home and subsequent photos of our work. The therapist shared her insight into the emotional issues directly related to the client's hoarding behavior, and discussed possibilities that might be standing in the way of progress. *She outlined behavioral techniques for me to use.* We discussed how I could reinforce the therapy and she could reinforce the organizing goals. I kept session notes recording our progress and backsliding to discuss in therapy. I made these notes available to my client. The notes made it easy to analyze what specific methods worked and what needed tweaking. The client also initiated a change in medication with her psychiatrist. Her decision-making improved and she said it was easier for her to detach herself emotionally from her possessions.

My client was able to get support from her family and friends. She was able to host a party at her home and invited people that had not been in her home *for over fifteen years*. This was a huge and joyous step for my client. It made me very proud and honored to have had the opportunity to work with her.

Put Community Service Agencies On Your Team

There is a whole roster of community service agencies that come up against the issue of hoarding. These agencies can provide resources for your hoarding client, including therapy referrals, evaluating the safety and health risks, housecleaning services, temporary housing, and medical assistance. The trick is finding the "go-to person." It is hard work to find the right person to talk to but is it possible. If one of these agencies has referred the client to you, your job is much easier. It means your client is already "in the system" and has met whatever eligibility requirements there are for access to these services. If your client is self-referred, be aware they may need to apply to be eligible for certain services, the details of which go beyond the scope of this book.

Community Service Agencies
- Federal Area Agency on the Aging
- Older Adult Mental Health Program
- Older Adult Protection Services
- Adult Protective Services
- State Department of Social Services
- Department of Children and Family Services
- Department of the Elderly
- Department of Housing
- Senior Adult Services
- Animal Control
- Sheriff's Department
- Fire and Rescue
- County Board of Mental Health
- Environmental Protection Agency

Hoarding Abatement Team and Hoarding Task Force

If your county or city is very lucky it will have a Hoarding Abatement Team or a Hoarding Task Force. A hoarding task force or abatement team is an official effort of representatives of various community agencies to educate, advocate and assist first responders, social service providers and the community about hoarding. Consider the mission of the Hoarding Task Force of Hampshire, Hampden & Franklin Counties in Massachusetts. It is pretty typical of the mission of most such abatement teams and task forces: *The Task Force seeks to develop a coordinated response among community agencies to the problem of hoarding, including providing information, referral resources and community programming designed to effectively deal with this problem in a sensitive and responsible fashion.*

An abatement team or task force brings together those "go-to people" I was talking about earlier but there is no uniformity of agency participation in these task forces. For example, the Fairfax County, Virginia task force's member agencies include the Health Department, Fire and Rescue, Department of Family Services (Adult and Child Protective Services), the Fairfax-Falls Community Board of Mental Health Services, the Office of the County Attorney, the Departments of Housing and Community Development, Planning and Zoning, Public Works and Environmental Services, and the Sheriff's Office. Other efforts, like the one in Seattle, are headed up by professional organizers and volunteers from disparate community groups and the general public.

Hoarding task forces range in size from a handful of community members meeting informally to large, formalized government-sponsored groups with their own web sites.

Maintaining a task force or abatement team is too expensive for many jurisdictions that cannot afford to remediate every hoarding situation given tight budgets. Gail Steketee, a renowned psychologist in the field of hoarding notes that, "Local officials are sometimes hesitant to step in, cognizant that a full-blown professional abatement can cost a county or city government upwards of

$50,000 each." It would be interesting to research whether a professional organizer's involvement with an abatement team or task force makes these projects more cost-effective, lowering the cost to government. As of now, there is no central clearinghouse for hoarding abatement teams and task forces, and no standard protocol on how to start one. A link to a listing of hoarding task forces is in the **Resources** section, but it is unknown how often it is updated.

Put Other Organizers On Your Team

Your local chapter of the National Association of Professional Organizers (NAPO), and members of the National Study Group on Chronic Disorganization who live near you, are the best sources of organizers. All organizers, who seek certification, take introductory courses about chronic disorganization where they learn about disorganization as a quality of life issue. Organizers also learn the importance of being non-judgmental, and they learn methods that work with people who need an unconventional approach to organizing. All of this education, in my opinion, is applicable to people who hoard and is adequate for Level I households. At Level II, I prefer that the organizers who work with me be NSGCD members, which assures me they have even more education. If they have not taken classes or read books about hoarding, I will provide a book to them. At Level III or higher, I require the organizers on my team to have worked with at least one person who hoards, and be an NSGCD member, preferably one pursuing a certificate in hoarding.

You may not live in an area where there is a NAPO chapter or NSGCD members. If you are inexperienced and more advanced organizers do not live nearby, a severely hoarding client might not be one to take on. Or you can improvise. A professional organizer in this predicament told me she hired two organizers from another state to drive in, one more senior than her and the other about the same level of experience. She paid for their (cheap) hotel, and they participated in the project for the educational value.

Put Family and Friends on Your Team

Family members and friends of your client can play valuable, supportive roles in a hoarding project. They must be willing to take your lead on what to do, be respectful of your client's feelings and their prized possessions, honor teamwork, and not be critical or impatient. It is my experience that family and friends really want to help. They just need direction and boundaries. Give them specific tasks to do:

- Make phone calls for therapy appointments, equipment rental, or arranging for a thrift store pick-up
- Sit and sort with the client
- Provide temporary housing during the de-cluttering or cleaning process
- Temporarily store valuables or other possessions until it is safe for them to be moved back into the house
- Assist with bill paying, grocery shopping, banking, laundry and other regular activities and errands during the project or afterwards on an on-going basis
- Chronicle the hoarding project by taking photos or video with the permission of the client

- Help clean, paint, decorate or otherwise beautify the home after the clutter is removed
- Transport donations and recycling to their respective recipients
- Help pay the bills for organizing, therapy or other services

Put a Geriatric Care Manager and/or a Social Worker On Your Team

Lynn Mino offers this advice if there is no task force in your area. "I think one of the best connections one could develop would be with a Geriatric Care Manager (**www.caremanager.org**)." Professional Geriatric Care Managers (PGCMs) are health and human services specialists who help families care for older relatives, while encouraging as much independence as possible. The PGCM may be trained in any of a number of fields related to long-term care, including, but not limited to, nursing, gerontology, social work, or psychology, with a specialized focus on issues related to aging and elder care. The PGCM acts as a guide and advocate -- identifying problems and offering solutions. Like PGCM's, social workers also have a wide variety of training and specializations. Some of them have training in CBT. Depending on their training, social workers (www.socialworker.com) can:

- Provide referrals for medical and mental health evaluation
- Consult and collaborate with other service providers and agencies
- Assess for mental capacity
- Coordinate overall care

Lynn Mino is a member of an association of women health care professionals. Several of those women have stepped forward to be available to Lynn for her clients in need of physical or mental health care. The National Study Group on Chronic Disorganization (NSGCD) has a roster of related professionals in social work, psychology, psychiatry, and nursing who can consult with you about your client.

Put Supplemental Service Providers On Your Team

You can't anticipate every service you might need. Every hoarding project is different. But you can depend on needing a super-duper housecleaning service and a licensed, but affordable repairman. People who hoard are particularly nervous about service people coming to their home. They fear being told on to the landlord or the condo association or other people with the authority to evict them. This is a righteous concern.

I make the service providers who work for me aware that the client's needs are special and that there is a plan in place for addressing the hoarding. In the meantime, I ask that they keep confidential the condition of the client's home. As I've said before, you'll be surprised how many service providers already know about hoarding.

It is smart to have service providers sign a simple form absolving you of any liability for injury or damages. A sample of this form is in **Appendix II**. By the same token, don't expose service providers to situations that may causes injury or damages. One of the best services you can procure from a community service agency is someone to evaluate safety prior to contracting service providers or you can add a private inspector or contractor to your agreement to cover this. You might also want to see if your client has a proper homeowner's insurance. When you seek special training for working with people who hoard, the legal implications of this kind of work will be more fully explained to you.

The best source for supplemental services is your local chapter of NAPO. NAPO organizers have already tried them out for quality and value, and likely for sensitivity! Or contact an NSGCD organizer with hoarding experience. Perhaps they have used a national service with local franchises or offices (such as ServicePro™). Or go to the good old yellow pages and screen them yourself. Here are some suggestions:

- pest control
- mold and mildew mitigation
- handyman/woman
- appraiser
- carpenter
- electrician
- HVAC repair
- thrift store pick up
- yard worker

- recycling drop off centers
- clerical support
- bookkeeper
- mobile shredding company
- exterminators
- housecleaning service *(look for the terms "decontamination," "sanitize," "deep clean" in the yellow pages ad)*
- dumpster company *(sometimes called "trash removal," "container company," "debris removal," or "hauling")*

Collaboration is a Two-Way Street

Katherine Anderson, the current president of the NSGCD, tells a story about a hoarding client who had hundreds and hundreds of old newspapers. Knowing them to be a fire hazard, she recruited the local Fire Marshal's help. Once a year the fire department offers free fire inspections. Dressed in his full fire marshal uniform, the fire marshal knocked on Katherine's client's door offering a free fire inspection. He talked her into letting him in, was very non-judgmental and did not let on that this was Katherine's idea. "We're just making a run through the neighborhood", he said. In no time at all, he convinced her to let go of 25 years of newspapers by declaring them an official fire hazard. Katherine was able to follow up by discarding them.

Lynn and Mo's relationship with one county fire marshal has spread to surrounding county fire marshals and code enforcers. The reputation and credibility of professional organizing is being spread along with it. "This is a wonderful opportunity to promote professional organizing, NSGCD and our education and certification process," notes Lynn.

An organizer gains much by teaming up with a collaborating therapist. No therapist wants to utilize their special training by being knee-deep in clutter. We're the pro's in that area. Also, the most effective therapeutic methods such as Motivational Interviewing and Exposure with Response Prevention are done "in-vivo", that is, on-site at the home, not at the therapist's office.

Perhaps in the future professional organizers can be trained in these techniques, lowering the cost of overall care. This may be a tall order. Even advanced psychology students who work as interns to therapists, are challenged in working with hoarding clients. In some states, adjunct assistants to therapists are prohibited. In others, only students taking coursework in clinical psychology programs can assist therapists. Still, the ground is broken and obstacles today may fall tomorrow.

The Self-Help Approach

It is the rare person who hoards, especially a severe hoarder, who can turn their life around without professional support. The challenges are so formidable and the progress so slow and difficult that it is easy to become demoralized and give up. Live self help and support groups, self-help books and online self-help groups under certain circumstances can be very beneficial to your client. The powerful combination of taking full responsibility for changing one's life and the support of a group of people with similar issues seems to work for some people who hoard. Sandra Felton knows this first-hand and refers to herself as a former hoarder.

Self-Help Groups and Support Groups

Sandra Felton is the founder of Messies Anonymous (MA), an organization that maintains face-to-face support groups, online support groups and a newsletter that reaches a combined total of 40,000 people. It is unknown how many are compulsive hoarders, but Sandra is convinced compulsive hoarders pass through MA doors. She says:

> "It's all about self-help, that this is 'my' responsibility. 'I' am the one who needs help. Nobody can do this for me. We like to encourage independence in the groups. Our motto is 'You alone can do it, but you can't do it alone.' We understand people are scared so it is a method designed for people to do it anyway, even when they are afraid. People are encouraged to start with baby steps, encouraged to share tips and ideas and stories and successes, and encouraged to take on small challenges like sticking with sorting through papers for 15 minutes. You can't have too much encouragement. The process of change really belongs to them and with active involvement and commitment it really works. But it is a long-term process."

Research on the efficacy of self-help-aided treatment for compulsive hoarders is promising. A 2007 article in *Society for Social Work and Research,* authored by Jordana Muroff, Gail Steketee, Joseph Himle and Randy O. Frost, explores the potential of Internet therapy.

They acknowledge that while CBT is moderately effective, therapists trained in this approach are "extremely limited." They studied the effectiveness of "…existing private unpublished stable ongoing online CBT-based group intervention designed for people with compulsive hoarding." Their conclusion is that such self help efforts "…may be helpful in relieving symptoms, building motivation, and reducing loneliness" and that these online group "…may extend access to mental health care, compliment existing evidence." Clearly more research is needed and online support groups are not a substitute for on-site or in-person therapy, but it seems that online assistance may be an alternative in certain circumstances.

Messies Anonymous conducts two online

moderated groups related to hoarding and the discussion revolves around group-determined topics. Participants receive awards for reaching levels of achievement.

Messiness-and-Hoarding at http://health.groups.yahoo.com/group/messiness-and-hoarding. Description: most disorganized people tend to keep too many belongings. This site does not intend to deal with the ordinary problem of keeping too much experienced by many. It is only for those for whom hoarding is a very significant problem either for themselves or loved ones and is not intended as a site for general use.

Friends of Hoarders at http://health.groups.yahoo.com/group/Friends-FamilyofHoarders-Clutterers/. Description: this group is for those who care about someone who is a hoarder. It is not a therapy group. Here we share information which may be useful in understanding those whose lives are impacted by hoarding.

Messies Anonymous can also be found at http://www.ma.com.

Ann Gambrell has been operating face-to-face (as opposed to online) self help groups called clutter support groups for over eight years. She is certain that over the years her participants have likely included all ranges of hoarding individuals. Ann explains the effectiveness of her groups this way, "I tell them I have seen it all and there is nothing they can tell me that will shock me." It is enormously helpful to know how clutter and disorganization looks in the lives of other people with similar problems. This understanding that they are not "the worst" and that there are others like them, builds trust and lays the groundwork for opening up to the group process. In contrasting groups with individual treatment, Dr. Frost notes that "...we have found that people make more progress in individual treatment.... But we have also seen individuals in groups bond together. They start to take care of one another, and they want to come to group, even if they are not working on the problem... group treatment keeps them motivated and going."

Success stories are key. Participants learn from

true testimony of current group members or past members, the changes they made in their life. They also learn it takes work and doesn't happen overnight. It takes commitment.

The groups are structured and revolve around specific, relevant topics like goals, routines, systems, purging, sorting, emotions, and de-cluttering. Commitments to small, realistic goals are made and reported on at each group and backsliding is compassionately addressed.

"Group members tell us they had family visit for the first time in ten years, or sat at the dining room table for a meal for the first time ever, or that the guest room was cleared out and the grandkids stayed over... I have also had clients who were not ready, dropped out and promised to return and didn't, or dropped out without notice but many stay on and progress," Gambrell reports. Her company, Creative Time-Plus can be reached at info@creativetimeplus.com or 310-212-0917.

Self-Help Books

Specialists on hoarding who have treated people in their clinics are making their treatment methods accessible, as much as practically possible, via self-help books. Even with the best medical care available, cure rates for people who hoard are not high, but some self-help programs have provided substantial improvement. Even the most authoritative self-help books advise therapy if the program is too hard to manage, the program fails or other emotional issues are an obstacle. I use self-help books in a variety of circumstances. I give them to organizers who assist me on simple hoarding projects but have no direct experience. They are also useful for clients who:

- Need to build a trusting relationship with you step-by-step. Reading these books together can be a great first step. The self-assessment quizzes and questionnaires in the books help you and your client establish a dialogue and build trust.
- Feel they must try things on their own before they'll collaborate with others. Accepting help is a big step for some people. They may want to exhaust all other approaches first.
- Want to understand the problem intellectually before they'll do anything about it. The books are informative, easy-to-understand and authoritative, and lead even the hardcore intellectual to action.

- Are looking for assurance that others have the same problem they do. The reader can easily identify with the anecdotes and information in the book. Once assured they are "not the only one," they will often accept help.
- Cannot afford mental health or organizing services. These books are inexpensive for the person with even limited funds.
- Have fears and social phobia so profound that interaction with others is not viable.
- Need to build confidence. People are inspired by the stories of other people and encouraged by the books.
- Are in therapy but their therapist doesn't know much about hoarding.

Buried in Treasures: Help for Compulsive Acquiring, Saving and Hoarding by David F. Tolin, Randy O. Frost and Gail Steketee in my opinion, is the most comprehensive self-help program. It is comprised of:

1. Scientific information for understanding of compulsive hoarding and how it personally affects the individual. A series of self-assessment questionnaires are used to achieve this goal.

2. Instructions for clearing living spaces and utilizing living space for its intended purposes
3. Strategies for preventing clutter from recurring
4. Organizing advice for storing possessions and documents
5. Strategies for improving decision-making
6. Methods for reducing compulsive buying and acquiring
7. Ways to identify and change unreasonable beliefs and manage emotional attachment
8. Problem-solving skills
9. Detecting warning signs of non-productive thoughts, feelings and behaviors and ways to intervene on them using new problem-solving skills

The organizing advice for removing clutter from the premises is practical, and the book gives credence to professional organizing noting that "... we think that professional organizers can be a very useful addition to your [the hoarder's] team, particularly organizers in the NSGCD with a chronic disorganization and/or hoarding specialty." In fact the authors of the book attribute some of the methods they use in treatment, to the work of professional organizers."

Overcoming Compulsive Hoarding: Why You Save and How You Can Stop by Fugen Neziroglu, Jerome Bubrick, and Jose Yaryura-Tobias also provides a good, basic education about hoarding and cognitive strategies for addressing it. Its language is slightly more technical than *Buried in Treasure.* On the other hand, the self-assessment tools are shorter. The organizing program for cleaning up clutter and keeping it clear is solid.

However, the book's perspective on professional organizing is mistaken. They mistake professional organizing with doing the organizing for the client and thus undermining their ownership of the organizing process and the process of change. This is a common mistake about organizing and one our profession will encounter again and again until we work hard enough to correct it.

Dr. Gail Stekette and Randy Frost also have a helpful book called *Compulsive Hoarding and Acquiring: Therapist Guide* and a companion *Client Workbook.* Though meant to be carried out under the guidance of a skilled clinician who has been trained in its use, and therefore not really a self-help book, both books provide many wonderful exercises you can do with your clients.

The Clean Slate Approach

I've heard family members threaten, in their anger and frustration, to "throw everything away" when it comes to dealing with a loved one who hoards. They may even try to recruit you into this scheme. I must say, I do understand the frustration. Often, the family has very good intentions, wanting to save the life of their loved one.

Remember that the "mish-mosh" of clutter contains valuables, and new or perfectly usable stuff along with the valueless clutter. "Overlooking this fact has caused considerable difficulty for hoarders who have been 'cleaned out' by the health department or housing authority or even by relatives," observes Dr. Frost. Confrontational tactics like the clean slate approach can "… spectacularly fail to resolve underlying pathology while instigating family conflict. Besides, such efforts are futile — the clutter returns," Frost continues.

Few people understand this better than Kristin Bergfeld whose company Bergfeld Estate Clearance Services has been dealing with people who hoard for decades. "We clear and reconfigure their homes in collaboration with family members, social workers, guardians, attorneys, and building managers as well as community and public agencies. We provide effective, comprehensive, and sensitive assistance. Unless carefully managed, the client's transition to an orderly home can be a distressing and even humiliating experience." Kristin has many great stories of buried treasure, including two dozen loose diamonds wrapped in brown, crinkly wads of Kleenex found in an old, dilapidated and crumbling suitcase.

Another reason this approach is not advised, says Dr. Jerome Bubrick, a co-author of the book *Overcoming Compulsive Hoarding*, is because "… such an approach can be very threatening to the hoarder who ties their identity to their clutter. A 'fresh start' forces a new identity on a person."

Rarely is a person ready for such a radical change without a lot of psychological support. And, finally, such an approach "...provokes feelings of loss, grief and maybe anger, plus when you wipe the slate clean you are doing it for them and they learn nothing new," concurs Dr. Renae Reinardy, a nationally recognized expert in the treatment of compulsive hoarding. A supportive, more gradual method is best (unless the situation is life-threatening.)

Toward "Best Practices"

We are not quite to a point where best practices for hoarding projects can be declared. This will require more pooling of the front line experience of our organizers who regularly work with hoarding clients. But from interviews with many organizers about their approaches, elements common to all emerge.

Respect Your Client

As with all clients, but especially those who are chronically disorganized and hoarders, be compassionate, encouraging and respectful. Being disorganized can make a person feel stupid, crazy, incompetent, embarrassed, angry, frustrated, exposed and vulnerable. Understand that letting you in is a big step. Slow down. Check in with your client often. A simple "How you doing?" every now and then can mean a great deal. And you can't say enough "Nice job," "Good idea" and "You can do it."

Respect your client's views, even if you disagree. My client, Margaret was sure she would one day get into a size 8 and wanted to keep all her clothing (some 500 pounds of it). I could not imagine her losing that much weight. Her current clothing size is 1X. "If you lose that much weight, you deserve new clothes!" I said. "Let's keep 100 pounds of the best clothes no matter the size," I suggested. Compromise and negotiations work with all but the most severe hoarders, especially if you quantify it.

Introduce your client to your assistants, service personnel; anyone who comes into their home. It is, after all, their home. Take care of their property. I've tumbled many a stack over with a hearty "Timber!" That's okay (usually). But treat hand-picked valuables with respect, cushioning them and stowing them out of harm's way.

Discuss the Team Process With the Client

Most clients are relieved that there is a proven, comprehensive approach that takes the matter seriously and addresses it compassionately. Share with your client an overview of the team approach as it relates to their project. Don't overwhelm them with detail. One organizer spells out each project phase on a piece of paper. Nothing fancy. Just the facts. Remember, they are already overwhelmed.

OUR PROCESS

Step One – Two organizing sessions alone with me

Step Two – Organizing session with me and my team

Step Three – Home visit by the therapist

Step Four - Etc.

Keep your client in the loop as to where you are in the process.

Be Clear As to Whom You Are Accountable

Hoarding clients are not all self-referred. In fact the more severe the case, the more likely there are other parties already involved. You may find yourself accountable to a family member, a conservator, an executor of an estate, a fire marshal, a neighborhood association or condo board, or family court, bankruptcy court, or housing court. It's not possible to spell out each scenario.

Determine who you are accountable to for progress and deadlines. Your contract/agreement should spell out how and to whom you will report progress. This might be photos, a third-party verifying the progress, or a simple report. Lynn and Mo recount that, "In many cases, we report to several different individuals. As part of the contractual agreement the client must give their permission for us to speak with the fire marshal or the related professional who referred the client to us." Accountability and cross-communication go hand in hand.

Be Clear About How You Will Be Paid

When an individual, either the client or a third party, pays you out of pocket, it is called "private pay." You may want to ask for a retainer for private pay services; that way you are paid substantially up front and the remainder monthly. A sample retainer agreement is in **Appendix II**. If your client meets certain eligibility requirements, some of the tab may be picked up by public (governmental) funds. Getting paid by the government can take 30 to 90 days.

Be Clear On Your Role In the Process

If the role of the organizer in a large, complex hoarding project sounds something like a project manager, you are right. A hoarding project takes a lot of preparation, planning and personnel. It has a timeline and a budget. The team needs supervision and communication. Somebody has to monitor progress. And the client's needs have to be managed appropriately. It is not advisable for you to play every role and wear all the hats. Be sure there is clarity as to everyone's role, especially yours!

Roles An Organizer Can Play In a Complex Hoarding Project

- Do hands-on organizing
- Consultant on the project (make a plan of action) but not do hands-on work
- Assemble the team
- Supervise the project

Get It In Writing

Written agreements and contracts convey to your client that there are other people just like them, and that you're relationship with them is business-like. Objectifying things in this way relieves a lot of stress of believing they are the 'only one' like this or the 'worst one'. It also serves to remind the client that your relationship, so exceedingly helpful, is not, however, personal.

When your client signs an agreement, it gives you both a way to converse about the situation, again objectifying the matter. Agreements and contracts appropriately make decisions the responsibility of the client, not the organizer.

And finally, written agreements and contracts clarify who is responsible for what so that it does not become grounds for arguments or friction. It's there in black-and-white protecting both your interests.

Document the Process

Try to obtain permission to take photos using a simple permission release form (see **Appendix II**). Assure them no personal identifiers such as their picture on the wall or documents with their name on it, will appear in the photos. It's a great way to:

- chart progress
- indicate problem areas
- enhance insight
- share with therapists
- prevent backsliding

Bring "before and after" photos of other clients to show them they are not "the worst" (unless, of course, they are the worst!)

Keep notes. They're great for therapy sessions, to share (selectively) with the client as refreshers, to document progress and trouble-spots and to use as material for writing your book about hoarding!

Take Care of Yourself

I have a distinct memory of myself after my very first encounter with a person who hoards. I was dazed and appalled. I felt impotent and I wanted to cry. I had been with this client for three hours and it was painful, slow and unproductive work (or at least it seemed so to me.) I learned later that he, on the other hand, was quite happy with the progress. After the session, I drove to a park, sat under a tree and sipped a margarita. My hands were dirty and I wanted to take a bath. Next day, I formed the NSGCD. You don't have to go to this extreme but camaraderie is very important. While we must work hard to be non-judgmental with our clients, we are only human. Have a place to vent with your colleagues, a trusted friend or family member. Here are some of my self-care recommendations:

- I have a little prep ritual I do before a hoarding project. I eat a peanut butter and apricot jelly sandwich, gulp fresh air, stretch my back, flex my hands in my protective gloves, drink water, and strap on my lumbar belt. I leave the address where I am at on a note with a friend along with when I expect to be back. Find a prep ritual that suits you.

- We covered personal safety earlier in the book, but it deserves repeating. Pay attention to your intuition. Check out the environment. Tell someone where you are and when you'll be back. Bring a cell phone.

- You have to work at your client's pace but you don't have to rest at their pace. Rest when you need to. Take real breaks, away from your client. Walk or drive away for 15 minutes, longer if you need to eat. Your client needs time away from you too.

- Eat real food like fruit, V8 juice, yogurt, and nuts. Don't just eat caffeine and sugar.

- Organizing is not good exercise, even rigorous hoarding projects. You'll bend, stretch, pull, push, carry and schlep, but it's not sustained or patterned like exercise is so make sure you still exercise.

- Don't obsess the night before a big job. You have a plan. You have support. You are a good person. Go to sleep. After the day's session is over wrap up, make notes, and do something other than organizing like reading or socializing. Leave the job behind.

- Reward yourself for a job well done. Chocolate is always good.

Monitor the Acquisitions Side of the Equation

Be clever and vigilant in your methods and techniques about mitigating acquisitions. Stop the junk mail and catalogs (see **Resources** for more info), get your client on a yard sale diet.

Try some of the anti-acquisition techniques in the books *Buried in Treasures, Overcoming Compulsive Hoarding,* and *Compulsive Hoarding and Acquiring Workbook.*

Always Have a Maintenance Plan

Working with a hoarder is not a one-time thing. Like many other chronically disorganized clients, they will need on-going maintenance and follow up to keep ahead of this very tough problem of excessive acquisition and saving. Plan to come back regularly but don't plan on doing the organizing for the client, even in the maintenance stage. Their discard and de-acquisition decisions are very important for them to implement. With the clutter slowly clearing away, they have a fighting chance. Don't take it away from them. Be helpful but not disempowering. Put supplemental services in place such as on-going housecleaning. And on-going therapy cannot be underestimated. Here is where your time management skills can come into play. Help your hoarding clients make and keep a schedule of regular activities that support sustained success.

Conclusion—Improving Quality of Life

Organizers have much to contribute to improving the quality of life for people who hoard. We are the ones who know best how to transfer very traditional organizing skills, such as sorting and categorizing in conventional and non-conventional ways to people who are challenged by these skills. We are the ones who connect information processing with organizational skills that result in methods and techniques helpful to chronically disorganized clients of all kinds. We are the ones who remediate the organizing skills people are deficit in, though it is important for us to study further just how to do this with people who hoard. Every skill we know to improve decision-making, mitigate perfectionism, optimize memory, deal with inattention and distractibility, and build fundamental skills like prioritizing, sorting and categorizing are required for improving quality of life including safely and compassionately promoting discard, curtailing acquisitions, de-cluttering a home, and returning it to functionality.

Quality of Life Indicators

It would be worthwhile to be specific about what we mean when we say "quality of life" as it regards people who hoard. A Google search of "quality of life" will give you over 86 million hits! It is a huge concept defined in many different ways given the context in which it is being applied. It is used in every context from comparing different cities to determining when to not resuscitate a terminally ill patient. Catherine Roster, the Research Director of the NSGCD believes that "With the right context in place, Quality of Life measures would be another great tool for orga-nizers." I believe a helpful adjunct to the CHS would be a Quality of life instrument. It would be a way to "fill out" if you will, the daily, functional issues a person who hoards faces that cannot be totally expressed by exposure to health and safety risks, or environmental constructs. Such a tool might help detect hoarding behaviors that a large home or use of off-site storage units might obfuscate. It might also be useful in non-residential environments like offices. And it can be tied to a whole range of organizational skills issues, not just the impact of clutter.

What might a quality of life tool measure? If the context was people who hoard, it might include social issues like:

- Disruption of usual family and social activities
- Significant conflict with family members
- Significant conflict with neighbors
- Significant conflict with authorities at work (supervisors)
- Significant conflict with landlord, tenant association, condo association
- Social isolation

It could also measure functional disruptions due to poor organizational skills such as:

- Inability to sort and categorize, creating clutter and disorganization
- Difficulty weighing alternatives and making decisions, that in turn increases stress

- Perfectionism tendencies that cause action-paralysis
- Severe trouble prioritizing that leads to neglecting important tasks

Quality of life indicators are obviously tricky to construct and measure because they are more subjective than say, health risks and safety issues. Some may be observable. Others might be divulged in informal conversation. Still others can be detected with a trained ear. A self-assessment instrument might be the best tool. I leave the development of such a tool, and the decisions as to what it should include, to more qualified social scientists than myself.

There is much more we can do in the area of mitigation. What has to happen to mitigate a person who hoards with mild hoarding tendencies from becoming worse? What has to happen for a person with significant hoarding behaviors to stop a slide into hoarding so severe their very home is a danger to them? What is the collaborative role of the organizer in mitigation? Answers to these questions will surely provide opportunities for organizers to improve quality of life.

Another area of more study is hoarding in the business environment. In a world of unlimited information, paper-based and electronic, virtual and hardcopy; compulsive acquisition and saving of information takes on a whole new dimension. Behind that desk with papers heaped to the ceiling, hard-drives filled to capacity, e-mails in the thousands and offices clogged with documents are people suffering from the great burden of mal-adaptive beliefs and oppressive behaviors related to hoarding. Like the clutter of a home, some information, facts, documents and papers are valuable and some are worthless.

Organizers can begin to build a knowledge-base from their vantage point about this pheno-menon and begin to compare notes with our colleagues in the mental health field so we can start that multi-disciplinary approach hoarding in the business environment will no doubt require.

Working with hoarding clients is difficult and therefore extremely rewarding. It is a dynamic field filled with many opportunities for growth and discovery. Through your efforts, many people will be helped. I can't say how proud I am to be a part of this effort.

Appendix I - The Clutter Hoarding Scale

The Clutter/Hoarding Scale© is an evolving document that may have changed since publication of this book. To be assured you are using the most accurate information go to **http://www.nsgcd.org/resources/clutterhoardingscale.php**

NATIONAL STUDY GROUP ON
CHRONIC DISORGANIZATION

The NSGCD
Clutter Hoarding Scale

Official Organizational Assessment Tool

Level	Structure and Zoning Issues	Pets and Rodents	Household Functions	Sanitation and Cleanliness
I	All doors and stairways accessible	Normal household pet activity 1-3 spills or pet accidents evident Light evidence of rodents/insects	Clutter not excessive	Normal housekeeping Safe and healthy sanitation No odors
II	1 exit blocked 1 major appliance or regionally appropriate heating, cooling or ventilation device not working for longer than 6 months	Some pet odor Cat spray or pet waste puddles Light pet dander in evidence 3 or more incidents of feces in cat box Limited fish, reptile or bird pet care Light-to-medium evidence of comon household rodents/insects	Clutter inhibits use of more than two rooms Unclear functions of living room, bedroom Slight narrowing of household pathways	Limited evidence of housekeeping, vacuuming, sweeping Tolerable, but not pleasant, odors Overflowing garbage cans Light-to-medium mildew in bathroom or kitchen Moderately soiled food preparation surfaces

Level	Structure and Zoning Issues	Pets and Rodents	Household Functions	Sanitation and Cleanliness
III	Visible clutter outdoors Items normally stored indoors evident outside (TV, sofa) 2 or more appliances broken or not functioning Inappropriate and/or excessive use of electric and extension cords Light structural damage limited to 1 part of home; recent (less than 6 months)	Pets exceed local Humane Society limits by 1-3 animals, excluding well-cared-for puppy or kitten litter less than 4 months old Stagnant fish tank Poorly maintained reptile aquarium; odor and waste Bird droppings not recently cleaned Audible, but not visible, evidence of rodents Light flea infestation Medium amount of spider webs inside house	Visible clutter outdoors Narrowed hall and stair 1 bathroom or bedroom not fully usable; i.e. items stored in shower Small amounts of 1-2 obviously hazardous substances, chemicals, substance spills, broken glass	Excessive dust Bed linens, including pillow, show evidence of dirt, long time use . No evidence of any recent vacuuming or sweeping Heavily soiled food preparation surfaces Obvious and irritating odor Unused, full or odorous garbage cans Dirty or soiled laundry throughout house, exceeding 3 hamper-size baskets per bedroom

Level	Structure and Zoning Issues	Pets and Rodents	Household Functions	Sanitation and Cleanliness
V	Structural damage obvious in home Broken walls NO electrical power, except for rural homes not serviced by power companies No water connection No sewer, septic system nonoperational Standing water in basement or room Fire hazard, hazardous material or contaminants storage exceeds local ordinances	Pets dangerous to occupants and/or guests Rodents evident and in sight Mosquito or insect infestations Regional "critter" infestations; i.e. snakes in interior of home	Kitchen and bathroom unusable due to clutter Client sleeping elsewhere as house is not livable	Human defecation Rotting food More than 15 aged canned goods with buckled tops and sides

Appendix II - Sample Forms and Agreements

Sample Agreement for Residential Organizing*

(REPRINTED WITH PERMISSION OF SIMPLIFY YOUR LIFE®)

This agreement is made between _____the client, and__(business name)____ for the purpose of setting forth the terms and conditions of the project at her home at _____. To that end, we will clear-out, de-clutter and organize her home. Initial Objectives----are to meet the code violations , health codes and whatever else is deemed necessary, remove the fire hazards and make the home more comfortable, livable and healthful. This agreement shall remain in effect until the work is completed to the client's satisfaction and the county's satisfaction but may be terminated in whole or in part by either party, at any time. In case of cancellation, any unearned portion of the retainer will be returned or any unpaid amounts due will be paid.

The scope of the project shall be determined by agreement between the client and _(business name)_____
(*See attached Agreement regarding specific estimate.*)

The client will compensate _____(professional organizer's name) at the rate of _____ per hour for each hour utilizes on or off the premises completing, planning or administering the project. The client will compensate any other professional organizer at their rate up to _____per hour. A daily time log will be kept and provided to the client. The client will pay for necessary services such as hauling. Additionally, the client will reimburse us for consumable supplies. Invoices will be delivered upon completion of the project. After application of the retainer, invoices will be payable upon presentation.

_____ and the independent subcontractors are expressly not the client's employees and agree to indemnify and hold harmless the client from any claims for injury, disability, or death arising from any worker's compensation, employer's liability and from the provisions of law pertaining to such situations or claims. No conditions of employment are intended to exist.

The client agrees to indemnify and hold harmless __(company name)__ and the subcontractors from any claim arising from valued items accidentally discarded or perceived to have been discarded.

Signed and agreed to:

_____ Client   _____date

_____ (Business name)   _____date

_____(Signature)   _____date

* consult with an attorney regarding legal forms, agreements and contracts

Sample Combined Estimate and Retainer *

(REPRINTED WITH PERMISSION OF SIMPLIFY YOUR LIFE®)

Client : _____

Services to be provided: _____

_____

Beginning Date: _____ Target Completion Date: _____

COSTS (for each organizer)

Fees: $ ____ Per Hour for _____ hours = $ _____
Fees: $ ____ Per Hour for _____ hours = $ _____
Fees: $ ____ Per Hour for _____ hours = $ _____

                              Total = $ _____

Other Costs:

Bags: _____ @ $_____   = $ _____
Bins: _____ @ $_____   = $ _____
Boxes: _____ @ $_____   = $ _____
Dumpster/Hauling _____   = $ _____

             Total Other Costs $ _____

                 Grand Total $ _____

Advance retainer $ _____

Terms for balance weekly: $_____ per week

Notes, remarks, special provisions: _____
_____

_____ _____   _____ _____
 [your signature]   Date   [client signature] Date
Business name

_____   _____
Printed Name and Title   Printed Name and Title

* Get the advice of an attorney for any legal forms, agreements or contracts that you use. Here are some other helpful sample Retainer Agreement Clauses.

SERVICES: I am an independent contractor. I am not your employee. Within this Agreement I provide the service of [describe]

FEES: The retainer fee for the first month of service is $ [Monthly Rate] due upon signing this Agreement. We have agreed that [retainer Date] will be your month's start date. In exchange you will receive [Hours Per Month] of service during your month. I will not exceed these hours without your prior electronic or written consent. Payment is due by check. [avoid accepting credit cards if the person cannot manage debt] made payable to [your company name]. Your cancelled check is your receipt unless you ask for a paper receipt.

EXPENSES: Expenses such as [describe] are extra. I will bill you for expenses which will be due to be paid within 10 days of billing. [you may want to consider an extra travel fee if you drive far to get to your client.]

CONFIDENTIALITY STATEMENT: You may discuss or disclose my working relationship with anyone you choose. However, I will not knowingly discuss, disclose or communicate any information about your personal or professional information, documents, papers, possessions, files, condition of home, or health status without your prior electronic, verbal or written consent.

Sample Release of Liability*

(REPRINTED WITH PERMISSION OF SIMPLIFY YOUR LIFE®)

(Company name) _____an independent contractor, is expressly not an employee of (your company) _____ and agrees to indemnify and hold harmless (your company) _____ from any claims for injury, disability, or death arising from any workman's comp, employer's liability and from the provisions of law pertaining to such situations or claims. No conditions of employment shall exist.

Signed and agreed to:

_____Independent contractor   Date _____

_____Your name and your company name

* This release is used between your organizing company and any other organizing companies or service companies that you use. If you use a licensed, bonded and insured contractor/subcontractor/independent contractor, you do not need this release. Consult with an attorney regarding legal forms, agreements and contracts.

Sample Blanket Agreement

Client fully permits organizer to do the following tasks whenever they arise and without verification or discussion:

Dispose of:
   Spoiled food and food wrapping
   Swollen canned food
   Anything infested

Recycle:
   Magazines older than one year
   Newspapers older than three month
   Unopened credit card offer
   Plastic water bottles

Donate:
   Excess clothes hangers
   Old eyeglass frames

_____   _____

Signature   Date

Sample Commitment Agreement*

For the Period _____ (date) to _____(date)

I, [CLIENT] agree to:

1. Empty refrigerator of spoiled foods and permit my organizer to verify this

2. Ask _____(name of family member) to bring four feet of newspapers to Recycling Center

3. Go to only ONE yard sale, garage sale or flea market

4. Permit my organizer to hire someone to take the mattress on the porch to the dump for which I will be reimbursed, up to $35.00 by the client within one week.

5. Permit my organizer to shred, without verification, the papers/ document I have given her.

6. Attend any scheduled therapy sessions and permit the therapist to communicate with me if she/he thinks there is something relevant for me to know.

I agree to: (Organizer's name) _____

1. Verify removal of spoiled food from refrigerator
2. Arrange for the removal of mattress
3. Shred the papers [CLIENT] has given me

_____Client

_____Organizer

*I usually make these for periods of one organizing session to the next and post it on the bathroom door. I try to include at least one acquisition-curtailment activity, one therapy obligation, a family support task, and several client obligations in each Agreement. The more specific and quantitative the tasks are the more compliance there is.

[Reprinted with permission of FileHeads Professional Organizers]

Sample Goal Agreement*

1. Invite my grandson to visit by end of the summer.

2. Be able to move about unobstructed by fall.

3. Have someone clean my kitchen and bathroom in the fall.

4. Repair the air conditioner by beginning of summer.

_____ _____
Signature   Date

* I use this as motivation, to keep us focused and on task, and I post it on the back of the front door. It is different from the Commitment Agreement which is very task and time specific. The Goal Agreement is higher-level and broader than the Commitment Agreement with less detail.

Sample Safe Haven Agreement©

Organizer agrees to keep in a safe haven* the below items to protect them during the organizing/de-cluttering process. The organizer promises to return these items to the client's home at any time she/he requests it but preferably at the completion of the project.

- The "elephant lamp"
- Coffee can of coins
- Computer hard drive
- Grandma's linen table cloth (stained)
- Hand-blown glass clown (broken)
- Box of heritage photos

*Depending on what the items are , a safe haven may be an agreed upon shelf in the client's home, the trunk of a car, a mobile unit like a POD™, an off-site storage unit or a family or friend's home. Don't promise to protect them from damage, or theft or other events that may be beyond your control. Just promise to keep them out of harm's way during the organizing/de-cluttering process. You may want to take photos of each items to prove their condition upon storage so it is not disputed later.

[Reprinted with permission of FileHeads Professional Organizers]

Sample Photo Release*

I _____[Client name] grant to [your name and company name] _____the right to use photos of the interior and exterior of my home for educational and customer service purposes between myself, my organizer and my mental health practitioner only. The photographs become the property of _____ [your name and company name]. However, granting the use of these photos for any other purpose is not permitted without my permission. My name, address, image or any other identifiers will not appear in the photos.

I have read and understand the above:

Signature [client] _____

Printed name _____

Signature [you] _____

Printed name _____

* Consult an attorney whenever you are using a legal form, agreement or contract.

Sample Property Pass

To: [name of condo association or homeowner association or property management company, etc.]

I, _____ (name of client) hereby

authorize _____(business name) unlimited access to my residence at

_____ (address) _____
for the purpose of fulfilling a Residential Organizing agreement (available upon request).

(business name) _____ is authorized to access the premises to do cleaning, organizing, disposal, de-cluttering, moving possessions, arranging possessions, transporting recycling and donations, and other tasks as may be necessary to complete the project even in my absence.

_____   _____
Client or authorized agent   Date

[Reprinted with permission of FileHeads Professional Organizers ©]

Appendix IIII - Supplies and Equipment

Standard
Bottled Water
Germicidal wipes
Plastic gloves (some people prefer cloth or latex gloves)
Large, plastic lawn or leaf bags
Plastic garbage bags with drawstrings
Brooms
Dustpans
Rags
Baseball Cap (or any other hat that covers hair)
First aid kit
Closed shoes or sneakers
Long pants
Sorting containers (pop-up mesh bags, plastic bins, laundry baskets, etc.)
Paper towels
Paper shredder

Other Supplies and Equipment
Trash cans
POD™ or Bagster™ other portable container
Face masks, type N95
Snow Shovels
Dumpster

Resources

Books and Newsletters

Buried in Treasures: Help for Compulsive Acquiring, Saving and Hoarding by David F. Tolin, Randy O. Frost and Gail Steketee   ISBN 978-019530058

Overcoming Compulsive Hoarding: Why You Save and How You Can Stop by Fugen Neziroglu, Jerome Bubrick, and Jose Yaryura-Tobias   ISBN 978-1572243491

Compulsive Hoarding and Acquiring: Therapist Guide by Gail Steketee and Randy O. Frost, and companion *Client Workbook*   ISBN 978-0195300253

The Hoarding Newsletter published by New England Hoarding Consortium (electronic). To receive, send an email to adcresearch@harthosp.org or call 860-545-7039

Hoarding-Related Organization Websites

http://www.Children of Hoarders.com

http://www.Helping Hoarders.com

http://www.Messies Anonymous.com

http://www.Squalor Survivors.com

http://www.Reclaiming Dignity.com

http://www.Clutters Anonymous.net

http://www.OCfoundation.org

http://www.Hoarders.org

http://www.Instituteforliving.org/ADC/

Institute on Compulsive Hoarding and Cluttering
http://www.mha-sf.org/programs/ichc.cfm

Hoarding Tasks Forces

See a directory of state-by-state Hoarding Task Forces at
http://www.helpinghoarders.com/taskforces.html

Clutter Support Groups

Creative Time-Plus, info@creativetimeplus.com or
310-212-0917

Messies Anonymous
http://www.messiesanonymous.com

http://www.ClutterersAnonymous.com

Blogs

Maintenance-Free Mom
http://maintenancefreemom.blogspot.com/

A Hoarder's Son
http://hoardersson.blogspot.com/

http://squalorsurvivors.com/community/blogs/

A Chronicle Of Clutter
http://squalorsurvivors.com/community/blogs/a_chronicle/
default.aspx

HiddenMessyGal's Blog
http://squalorsurvivors.com/community/blogs/
hiddenmessygals_blog/default.aspx

My Path To Success
http://squalorsurvivors.com/community/blogs/
my_path_to_success/default.aspx

Taming My Jungle
http://squalorsurvivors.com/community/blogs/
taming_my_jungle/default.aspx

Lady Clutterbug
http://squalorsurvivors.com/community/blogs/
lady_clutterbug/default.aspx

Interactive Forums

Children of Hoarders
http://www.childrenofhoarders.com/forum/ and
http://health.groups.yahoo.com/group/childrenofhoarders/

Helping Hoarders
http://www.helpinghoarders.com

Messies Anonymous
http://health.groups.yahoo.com/group/Messiness-and-
Hoarding/

Squalor Survivors
http://squalorsurvivors.com/community/default.aspx

Reclaiming Dignity
http://reclaimingdignity.com

Clutters Anonymous
http://www.clutterersanonymous.net/

Organizations for Professional Organizers

National Study Group on Chronic Disorganization
http://www.nsgcd.org

National Association of Professional Organizers
http://www.napo.net

Board of Certification for Professional Organizers
http://www.certifiedprofessionalorganizers.com

Videos And DVD's

"Packed House" – contact Producer for more information
Jody Hammond, Independent Producer
1045 Cornish Dr.
Encinitas, CA 92024-5107
Office/Pager (760) 436-2780
Cell (619) 318-6926
lajody@cox.net

"Possessed" - Free, online at
http://www.vimeo.com/channelMPH/page:2 or copies can
be purchased at directly by contacting
Martin@MartinHampton.com. The DVD comes with other
short films about hoarding.

"Packrat" - Fanlight Productions at 800-937-4113 or
info@fanlight.com

"Help, I'm a Hoarder" - The Learning Channel (TLC),
available via YouTube video and is posted at
http://www.helpinghoarders.com/TLCvideo2007.html

"Seven Dumpsters and a Corpse" – view trailer at
http://www.messiemother.com/film
To purchase go to http://www.documentarychannel.com/
store/product_info.php?products_id=305

"The World of Compulsive Hoarders - via YouTube video at
http://www.helpinghoarders.com/Chan4_Video2007.html

"My Mother's Garden" – see the trailer at
http://www.mymothersgardenmovie.com/pages/trailer.html
Release set for Fall, 2008

"Grandma, the Packrat: New Approach Finds Pearls Amid
the Junk" http://www.bergfelds.com

Animal Hoarding

http://www.animalhoarding.com

http://www.psychiatrictimes.com/display/article/
10168/54031?pageNumber=2

Acquisitions Curtailment

To stop unsolicited junk mail—
http://www.dmachoice.org
http://www.privacyrights.org
http://www.greendimes.com

To stop unsolicited catalogs—
http://www.catalogchoice.org

To stop credit card and insurance offers—
1-888-5-OPTOUT

Compulsive Shopping information:
http://www.pubmedcentral.nih.gov/articlerender.fcgi?
artid=1805733

"Is My Brain Making Me Buy Things I Don't Need?"
Layton, Julie, January 20, 2007
http://www.HowStuffworks.com/brain-shopping.htm

"How to Manage a Compulsive Shopping Or Spending
Addiction"
http://www.indiana.edu/~engs/hints/shop.html

Consuming Passions: Help for Compulsive Shoppers, by
Ellen Mohr Catalano ISBN 978-1879237384

Organizations of Therapists, Social Workers, and Other Professional Services

Find licensed social workers with a specialty in OCD in your state. Ask if they have experience in hoarding.
http://www.socialworkers.org

To locate a geriatric care manager in your state—
http://www.caremanagers.org

To find a full-service, residential cleaning service, go to the Association of Residential Cleaning Services International at http://www.ascsi.org

To find therapists with training in cognitive behavioral therapy and experience with hoarding, go to The Obsessive Compulsive Foundation, http://www.ocfoundation.org or the National Association of Cognitive Behavioral Therapists at http://www.nacbt.org or contact your state mental health association for a referral.

Collaborative Therapy for Compulsive Hoarding© expert: Heidi Shultz, CPO-CD, 805-569-5288, organize@heidischulz.com

On-Going Research

If you or a family member has a clutter problem, the Anxiety Disorders Center of Hartford Hospital in Connecticut, under the direction of Dr. David Tolin, is recruiting family member pairs (parent/child, siblings, etc.) for an internet-based research study. Other research projects underway require in-person participation. For details about hoarding-related research call 860-545-7685 or go to:

David F. Tolin, Ph.D.
Anxiety Disorders Center
(860) 545-7685
dtolin@harthosp.org

Boston University, under the guidance of Dr. Randy Frost and Dr. Gail Steketee, are also researching hoarding. For details, call 617-353-9610 or go to:

Gail Steketee, Ph.D.
Boston University School of Social Work
(617) 353-3750
steketee@bu.edu

Randy O. Frost
Smith College
(413) 585-3911
rfrost@email.smith.edu

Level	Structure and Zoning Issues	Pets and Rodents	Household Functions	Sanitation and Cleanliness
IV	Structural damage to part of home (longer than 6 months) Mold or mildew on walls or floors Inappropriate use of appliance: storing nonfood items in refrigerator (beyond batteries, film) Evidence of damage to 2 or more sections of wall board Faulty weather protection: deteriorated or ineffective waterproofing of exterior walls, roof, foundation or floors, including broken windows or doors; missing or damaged gutters/downspouts Hazardous electrical wiring Odor or evidence of sewage backup	Pets exceed local Humane Society limits by 4 animals (any type) Obvious aged animal waste exceeding 2-3 recent "accidents" Pet dander on all furnishings Pet has free range with evidence of destructive behavior, clawed furnishings, chewed doors or frame Excessive spiders and webs Bats, squirrels, raccoons in attic or room Flea infestation	Designated bedroom unusable; using living area or sleeping on sofa or floor Hazardous materials stored inside of home, e.g., gasoline, aged, rusted and leaking paint or household chemical cans or bottles Excessive combustible and highly flammable packed material in living area or attached garage	Rotting food on counters 1-15 aged canned goods with buckled tops and sides No covers on beds, sleeping directly on mattress, lice on bedding or furnishings No clean dishes or utensils locatable in kitchen

About The Author

Judith Kolberg founded FileHeads Professional Organizers in 1988. Soon after, she published her first book, *Conquering Chronic Disorganization.* She is the recipient of the industry's highest honor, the prestigious Founder's Award from the National Association of Professional Organizers (NAPO). Her contribution to the inaugural certification program for professional organizers was recognized with the President's Award. She is the former President of the Georgia chapter of NAPO and has served as NAPO's Director of Professional Development. *Conquering* is a recommended text for the certification of all professional organizers and has sold over 80,000 copies in the US and Korea.

Kolberg is the founder of the National Study Group on Chronic Disorganization. Her second book, *What Every Professional Organizer Needs to Know About Chronic Disorganization,* launched an entire profession of organizers specifically dedicated to addressing the needs of individuals who are chronically disorganized. She served as the Director of the NSGCD for seven years and is the recipient of their highest honor, the Highlighter Award. *What Every Professional Organizer Needs to Know About Chronic Disorganization* is a required textbook for the certification of organizers specializing in chronic disorganization and has sold over 10,000 copies. *What Every Professional Organizer Needs to Know About Hoarding* is the second book of this series. Kolberg is pursuing a specialty certificate in hoarding from the NSGCD.

FileHeads clientele includes business owners, entrepreneurs, upper management and corporate executives from all over the country; and individuals with special organizing challenges including many people with Attention Deficit/ Hyperactivity Disorder or who are compulsive hoarders. In 2002, *ADD-Friendly Ways to Organize Your Life* was published by Routledge, an imprint of the Taylor & Francis, a worldwide academic press. It is co-authored with Dr. Kathleen Nadeau. *ADD-Friendly* has sold over 75,000 copies in the U.S., Canada, England, and the Netherlands.

Kolberg's depth of experience and humorous delivery has made her a popular corporate trainer and keynote speaker. She addresses audiences live, by teleclass and webinar on organization/disorganization related topics and has been covered in more than 60 print, TV and radio media outlets. Kolberg is also the owner of Squall Press, a small press that publishes some of her books.

She is a native of Levittown, New York and a graduate of the State University of New York at Binghamton with a B.A. in Sociology. She derives her organizing skills from her early career as a political organizer. Her political activism and a background in executive secretarial and corporate office management brought her to New York City where she often worked in the shadow of the World Trade Center. Deeply affected by the events of September 11th, 2001, she wrote *Organize for Disaster: Prepare Your Home and Your Family for Any Natural or Unnatural Disaster*. She holds a certificate in Community Emergency Response Team training and resides in Atlanta.

Other Products by Judith Kolberg

Books

Title Information	Book price	Ebook price
Conquering Chronic Disorganization ISBN 978-0-9667970-3-9	$14.99	$12.00
What Every Professional Organizer Needs to Know About Chronic Disorganization ISBN 978-0-9667970-2-2	$12.00	$7.00
Organize for Disaster: Prepare Your Family and Your Home for Any Natural or Unnatural Disaster ISBN: 978-0-9667970-4-6	$15.99	$13.00
ADD-Friendly Ways to Organize Your Life ISBN 1-58391-358-0	$21.95	Not Available

*e-Books are downloadable, searchable PDFs

MP3 recordings

All MP3 downloads are $8.00 each.
MP3 #1 Time Management, Time Perception and Adult AD/HD
33 min. 45 sec.

MP3 #3 The De-Acquisition of Stuff
36 min. 45 sec.

MP3 #4 Getting from 'Here' to 'There': Executive Function and Organizing
40 min. 04 sec.

Special Reports**

Available as hardcopy for $7, as digital download for $5.

#1 Time Management, Time Perception and Adult AD/HD

#2 Understanding Decision-Making, Procrastination and Perfectionism in Chronic Disorganization

#3 The De-Acquisition of Stuff

#4 Getting from 'Here' to 'There': Executive Function and Organization

**The Special Reports are not transcripts of the MP3's. They contain information not available in the MP3 such as endnotes, websites and other references. The MP3s are teleclass recordings, not transcriptions of the Special Reports. They contain information from a question and answer session that is not available on the Special Report. Together the Special Reports and the MP3 are the most complete information on the topics.

Bundles

All four Special Reports (hardcopy)	$22.00
All four Special Reports (digital download)	$20.00
All three MP3s	$20.00

Any single pair of corresponding Special Report and MP3	$12.00
All four digital Special Reports and all three MP3s	$40.00
ADD Package - ADD-Friendly Ways to Organize Your Life, and Special Report #1 (hardcopy only)	$27.00
Chronic Disorganization Package - Conquering Chronic Disorganization and Special Report #2 (hardcopy only)	$20.00
Certification Package - Conquering Chronic Disorganization (recommended for professional organizers exam) What Every Professional Organizer Needs to Know About Chronic Disorganization (recommended for NSGCD certifications and certificates)	$24.00

All are available for purchase online at http://www.SquallPress.com.

Special discounts are available on quantity purchases by corporations, association, and others. For details, please call Squall Press at **404-231-6172** or email info@squallpress.net

Printed in the United States
210187BV00004B/14/P

9 780966 797053